GRAPPLING

GRAPPLING

WHITE MEN'S JOURNEY FROM FRAGILE TO AGILE

ANDREW HORNING, MSW

LIONCREST
PUBLISHING

GRAPPLING
White Men's Journey from Fragile to Agile

ISBN		
	978-1-5445-1960-9	*Hardcover*
	978-1-5445-1958-6	*Paperback*
	978-1-5445-1959-3	*Ebook*
	978-1-5445-2107-7	*Audiobook*

CONTENTS

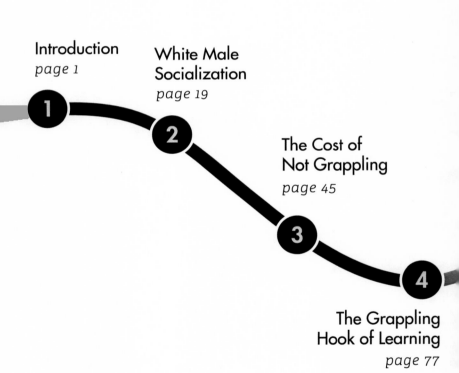

ACKNOWLEDGMENTS

To my parents: I'm grateful for so much, but perhaps top on the list is your value of showing up. You show up to your life with a passion and commitment that takes my breath away.

To my siblings: Missy, John, Joe—it's scary to love people as much as I love you, and I'm thankful that our ongoing work together has helped us re-write the story of our childhoods and we continue to learn and grow together.

To my extended family: Antonio, Mike, Fiona, Terry, Tristan, Nick, Brendan, Reed, Noah, Finn, Wiley. Thank you for what we create in our family gatherings, even if it's a bit uncomfortable as we sort it out together. And to David R. for your leadership and stewardship of HB and to Dara for leading HFF through huge growth, learning, and impact.

To men's group: Andy, Andrew, Burke, Chris, and Eric—Our every-other-week meetings for the last twenty years have so fed me and what it means to be in community together, what it means to be a man, that I can't imagine what my life would be like without you.

To 492 Broadway: Keith, Evan, Will and Kevin—I love our shared memories, date nights, and living together as we dealt with our first jobs right out of college. And we will miss you, Kevin. He was the best roommate Emily, Christian, and Carly.

To my friends: Joe and Allison, Molly, Mike, Bill, Lee, David, Paul, Brian, Will, Chris K., Coach G., the Mapleton Crew, and all those who attended the "dudes dinners." You remind me of that quote about friends who "know all about you, but like you anyway." Thank you for that.

To all my students, clients, and players over the years: I cringe sometimes at how I showed up, but I'm grateful for the mutual learning, your commitment to growth, and trust you gave me.

To all those I haven't been able to successfully grapple with over the years: friends and exes. Thank you for answering the call, and I'm sorry for my part in not getting to the other side.

To my Hoffman colleagues: it's a unique thing to spend such intensive time together during each process and I'm grateful for all that it births in my life and for each of you and our leaders Matt, Liza, and Raz.

ACKNOWLEDGMENTS

To the folks who helped with Grappling: Thank you for your expertise in getting this book out especially those at Scribe, most especially Sonia. The power of the written word is safe in your hands.

To my coaches and therapists: Martha and Dorian, you have helped our family so much. Sarah, I appreciate your guidance. Kap and Stuart, you loved me in those formative years and modeled for me what it means to be a man and how to help people on their own transformative journey.

To my core three: Genny, Campbell, Mackenzie. Our little pod is figuring it out and grappling with all that life is bringing us. I'm grateful for each of you and how you show up to your own life.

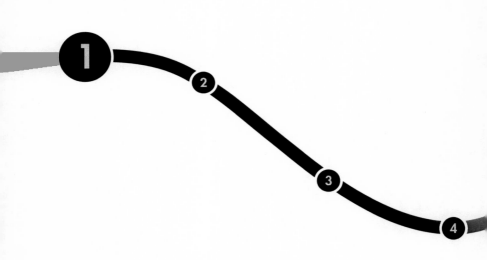

INTRODUCTION

"And the day came when the risk to remain tight in a bud was more painful than the risk it took to blossom."
—Anais Nin

I was born into a life of privilege. If there's a form somewhere that inventories who will have a head start in the race that is life, every box for me would be checked. I'm White. I'm male. I'm Christian. I'm straight. My family is wealthy, so I never have known what it is to have "hunger insecurity" or be "one paycheck away from homelessness." I'm educated, I don't have a criminal record, and I live in the United States, the developed country of my birth. I have a full Privilege Bingo card, for sure.

I have it made. I'm in the White male power structure club. The club does have its dues, though. It unfairly taxes society for its support, of course. But there's also an expectation that I'll give up big chunks of myself. The cost to White males shows up in basic things like reduced life expectancy, increased heart attacks and strokes, alcohol and drug abuse problems, happiness deficits, and suicides. Indeed, White men outdo all other demographics in suicide. In the "Healthy Men" column posted during October 2019 on Medical Xpress, author Armin Brott noted, "White men—especially those aged 25–64—are at least twice as likely to take their own lives as men in every other racial group except Native Americans, who lag white men by about 15 percent.... And white males, who make up about 30 percent of the population, account for nearly 70 percent of all suicides."

Why do we succumb to drink and drugs and deaths of despair and do so at increasingly higher rates than other demographic groups? When I look at myself in the mirror, considering the stats, I see a person who, despite all my privilege, is vulnerable and in a struggle with the side effects of my privileged life.

And behind all that is another cost to White men, something deeper and more tragic: it is the expectation that we jettison parts of our human core—a whole world of feelings, uniqueness, the skills to have thriving relationships, the strength to embrace courage, courage enough to allow the world to change us for the better. We have holes inside instead of wholeness. You see, the White male power structure club is founded on a principle of reduction. It seeks to reduce each member, narrowing, flattening, and draining the color out of our internal worlds, even as it excludes and penalizes everyone else for non-membership. It's like a pact with the devil, who expects our souls in return.

How does it make any sense that the club gives us the best chance of worldly success, wealth, and power while beggaring everything that fuels a rich inner life? How does it make sense to take from every other element of society to ensure the survival of the club? We can see all the grim ways the club exacts its cost to society. As reported in a September 2020 Citigroup report:

- Discrimination against African Americans cost the U.S. economy $16 trillion since 2000. And the GDP could gain $5 trillion through 2025 if only disparities in wages, education, housing, and investment were somehow immediately fixed.

- "Of the 3.1 million American adults estimated as banned from voting, 2.2 million are Black Americans." This is because half of U.S. states have enacted voting restrictions over the last decade.

- Discriminatory housing practices mean Black homeownership is nearly 50 percent versus White ownership, which is nearly 80 percent.

It's easy to find damning statistics:

- The U.S. National Academy of Sciences discovered in 2016 that nearly a third of White first-year medical students believed that blood coagulated at different rates for Blacks and Whites; and that about a fifth believed that Blacks have stronger immune systems.

- Mental Health America, noting that it, "understands that racism undermines mental health," reveals in its piece "Racism and Mental Health" that "when treating Black/African American clients, clinicians tend to overemphasize the relevance of psychotic symptoms and overlook symptoms of major depression compared to when they are treating clients with other racial or ethnic backgrounds. For this reason, Black men in particular are greatly over-diagnosed with schizophrenia—...four times more likely to be diagnosed with schizophrenia than their white male counterparts."

It's too easy to find such statistics in all the long years we've been studying our individual and institutionalized bigotry and failing to stop it. And I hadn't even started on statistics regarding sexism and outright misogyny.

And while these statistics continue stacking, it keeps quietly draining our internal worlds, our socialization leaving we men defenseless against failure. Sure, White men have a history of success in this country, but as legendary Los Angeles Dodgers manager Tommy Lasorda put it, "The only problem with success is that it doesn't help you deal with failure."

The current societal power structure dominates us all whether fortunate or unfortunate. It shapes and encodes us like a virus infiltrating and changing cells. And yet, we White males tend to hope that the world will always remain the same, just so that we don't have to change the way we are. And so that we can maintain our status atop the social order.

IT HURTS

Many of us know that whatever is going on—with certain people perpetually down and out no matter their deservingness while certain others enjoy buoyancy no matter their deservingness—we know it makes no sense at all in a moral, just universe. This is uncomfortable and disturbing for those of us benefitting from the status quo. And then we get uncomfortable and disturbed about feeling that way: Why should we feel guilty about our blessings, looking a gift horse in the mouth? People are supposed to get help and at least a couple lucky breaks in life, right? We all need it, and damn, if we didn't work hard to get where we are.

Anyway, *we didn't make the system*, we think. The system dictates that life comes down to dominator or dominated, victim or perpetrator, irrational women versus hyperrational men, and that it's all about who best takes advantage of the opportunities.

No matter what the system says, though, you know that reducing society into Black and White is simplistic. People aren't just categories, and our justifications for "how things are" feel incomplete if not hollow when we watch complex cause-and-effect play out on the television: White rapists still get away with it "because it would ruin his life to go to prison." Black men lie dead in streets across the nation with a uniform somehow shielding a White murderer. It's wrong. You know it. We all know it. But damned if we know what to do about it.

Our hearts can get twisted, and we don't know what to do with that either. We men like our solutions. Doing so rids of our uneasiness, discomfort, and helplessness. A solution would soften the shame many of us feel (or work hard not to feel) because we benefit from a society that puts White men on top while our excesses burden everyone else below. We don't want to have to think about any of this let alone feel bad. We're trying to live good, decent lives here.

In a different time, we didn't feel accountable for the injustices even if we knew enough to be self-conscious of our White male privilege. That time isn't coming back, nor should it. But that doesn't help us. We still have no idea how to be in a world that is unjust when we are the ones benefiting from the injustice. We cannot renounce ourselves, after all. We are always going to be White males. And there's nothing inherently wrong with that. It feels like a conundrum with no answer, and we feel defensive every time we are challenged. Which is a lot in these times.

The world is changing rapidly, and we can't keep up. There are times when we don't understand the hows and whys of all this change, and in our confusion, we don't know how to react. On occasion we end up projecting our insecurities onto others, or worse yet, we end up blaming the victims. One minute, we're mad at the violent police officer, the next minute, we're mad at Black people.

This outside pressure from the world is only going to get worse. Joining the front-of-mind issues of systemic racism and sexism are the pandemic and climate change crises. They threaten us with even less certainty and security.

The COVID-19 pandemic means sudden lockdowns and a host of unknowns and uncertainties. We retreat to our homes, trying to become hermetically sealed hermits. But then climate change strikes. When hurricanes inundate or fires rage, we must evacuate together, risking a deadly viral infection.

And, meanwhile, politics.

We react to it all according to our conditioning. Some try to dominate it before it can dominate them. Some dig in their heels, entrenched no matter the reality, denial a shield against the fear of losing something or even everything. Others will try to change pieces of the world because action can smother any unwanted feelings; just fix it and forget it—for a while at least.

But all these reactions don't make the problems of our world go away. Our coping mechanisms aren't coping at all, but instead are just a cycle of exposure, upset, ineffectual action, and brief symptom relief. And then we start all over again. It's an ulcer of the spirit, flaring up and causing pain, which we then treat with our own brand of snake oil. It won't fix us and may even do more harm.

There is a better way to meet the world. Psychologist Rick Hanson noted that, "When things fall apart around you, you're really left with what you've developed inside you." Grappling is the way to get there—the work that develops the you inside.

8·20·22
so true
for whats
happening
right
now

THE GIFT OF THE GRAPPLE

Things *can* start to make sense. And though this may sound trite, it all starts with you. That's good news. Unlike all the stuff "out there," you have a lot of control over yourself. You just have to be willing to grapple.

As a practicing therapist and then as a process teacher at the Hoffman Institute, I've spent years supporting people in change and transformation. This transformation takes grappling, which is defined as *engaging in a close struggle without weapons.* It is purposefully exposing yourself to discomfort—all to have that gradual or sudden rebirth, where you emerge stronger and better, and feel simultaneously a sense of power and humility. In this new state of being you'll gain more inner peace and a stronger emotional capacity, and that means more opportunity for getting all the things you want in your life—joy, meaning, connection, success.

But if, in fact, it gives you a new lease on life, why wouldn't more people raise their hands to do it, to grapple and to grow? Well, many don't know how. Especially White men whose privilege has allowed them to avoid the tough issues that women and minorities must grapple with, often on a daily basis as they navigate their lives. Good White, straight, Christian men may have learned the right values in their childhoods, but we won't have to face how our privilege belies those values as it hurts everyone else.

And because we hold positions of power and wealth—with Joe Biden's election, White men held forty-five out of forty-six presidencies while all but six Supreme Court justices in our entire history of 114 have been White men; and Whites held 85.5 percent of the country's wealth in 2019 (Federal Reserve)—because of all our power and wealth, we hold the reins. If we stay stuck, society stays stuck, stuck with the White male dominance dogma practiced all around us.

yes!

yes!

When White men who hold the levers of power start grappling, larger systemic change can happen. The goal is to grow into emotionally strong members of our communities, ready for the ongoing changes we'll face. Only then can we use our full Privilege Bingo cards to work toward the social change that is best for all of us instead of just reinforcing the status quo.

When White men who hold the levers of power start grappling, larger systemic change can happen.

BREAKING IT DOWN

This book teaches you about grappling with the king of perpetrators—the White male persona, especially the White, straight, Christian, cisgender male persona. You'll understand how you came to be conditioned to play your part—to live out a role that stifles the authentic you. You'll learn to take on the conditioning that's been buffeting you your whole life by learning how to grapple with yourself and the world around you. You'll walk away with a framework to comprehend today's world, and how to let it change you in ways that support a nimbler you. If businesses can position themselves as innovators, why can't we—*you*— consider that pivot, too? Become an innovator in your own life. Doing so will build an internal agility that will serve you handsomely for the rest of your life.

And you'll be able to leave behind a sanctified, white-washed emotional landscape. You can stop bleeding out your essence, that cost of staying in White Male character. You'll learn to embrace your own core instinct, your authenticity, and a self-compassion that allows for mistakes, giving you the full range of your humanity. You'll learn how to draw lines between your internal world, your relationships, and our society. And to do all this, you'll also learn to be open to learning. Remember when that used to be fun, an adventure in new discovery?

I want you to leave behind denial, stonewalling, and anger, to instead feel lighter, liberated, and able to respond in a way that acknowledges all of the different colors of the world. Instead of saying "life should be easy," I want you to acknowledge that life is hard. Instead of focusing on being right, I want you to focus on *getting* it right.

I want society to change because of your work and how you show up in the world, and research has shown this is possible: it takes just a quarter of the population to influence change in an entire population, according to 2018 research published in *Science* magazine. Just one quarter! When it comes to change, it doesn't take all of us, it just takes some of us. You're going to be one of those movers and shakers.

As writer Margaret Mead said, "Never doubt that a small group of thoughtful, committed citizens can change the world: indeed, it's the only thing that ever has."

THE NEED IS GREAT

During the writing of this book, powerful events occurred calling us to rewrite the story of what it means to be a white man. Rioters invading the Capitol building in an insurrection is an indictment of how we are dealing with the changing times. George Floyd's murder is another example. The images of his murder, of a man's face being pressed into the ground, the life slowly seeping out of him while he said, "I can't breathe" and called out for his mother—the images haunted people all over the world.

For me, the wrenching, slow-motion death of a human being contrasted to the White man unflinchingly kneeling on his neck was a potent metaphor for White male privilege.

White male privilege dehumanizes everyone, including White men themselves. The officer knelt, hands in his pockets, expressionless, a mask where his humanity should be, an automaton carrying out programming.

In those moments, as a dying Mr. Floyd struggled for air, who had more life? Mr. Floyd or his murderer? I would argue that Mr. Floyd had more life. Even as he couldn't find his breath, we saw his humanity. We could see the heart of him, even as his heart was stopping, and the heartlessness of the man killing him. We could see George Floyd's essence: George Floyd, a living human being.

There was no life in the man who killed him. It's hard to kill people, but if you don't have any life inside you, it makes it a lot easier. In his callous act, we find a perpetrator who allowed himself over the course of his lifetime to become dehumanized, a would-be White hero influenced by role models in popular media—those lawmen and soldiers who save the world from people not like "us." As a child, he might have watched heroic White men shooting "savages" in a Western, defending stolen land. And so it is for us White men, conditioned to think ourselves heroes, conditioned to compete and to dominate, conditioned to forget to some degree or another, our humanity. We all suffer from Jason Bourne Syndrome, capable of things we were not born to do, conditioned by society to some degree or another to become dehumanized in favor of a role: White Male, not White male *human being*.

I've learned to grapple with my own White male identity. I continue to do so on an ongoing basis. I've confronted parts of my past, and my life is much fuller and richer because of it. I'm writing this book because I have the experience of being in the transformation space, helping people change. And I've done lots of, as a friend and colleague described her efforts, "interrogating my Whiteness." My hope is that you reclaim your wholeness, to open up the parts of you long hidden away, and to know what it is to live more fully, more richly, more truly. I want you to be the strong, living, vital man you were born to be.

In my professional life helping people navigate the process of getting more of what they want in their lives, I've seen how they develop a better relationship with change—change around them and change inside them. I teach them how to grapple and watch them put down their defenses and self-punishment, sometimes lifetimes of accumulated weight. In doing so, they become lighter and open up as they once did, before society loaded them down with its demands. I want to do that for you: help your spirit burn fierce again.

WHAT THE BOOK IS AND ISN'T

Despite our socialization, we all have a spirit inside of us. I see it come alive again and again in teaching the Hoffman

Process. "The Process" helps people transcend issues and patterns of behavior that keep them alienated from their own inner selves. Seeing them emerge from underneath their limiting patterns is perhaps one of the most beautiful things I'll ever see. It's compelling and moving to witness people show up in their essence. This book is intended to help you reconnect with your own essence, to connect with your spirit and find your inner strength and vitality. This is the authentic you, the one who resides underneath all the ways you've been socialized as a White male in this society. Owning the ways in which you have been taken from you is the first step in reclaiming yourself, starting with the campaign that makes war on boys' emotions.

This will ask a lot of you. It will ask that you bring courage and compassion to this journey. This isn't a book about blaming or shaming. Yes, White men have victimized whole peoples for too long without being held accountable. But we have been indoctrinated into this victimizer role, inheritors of a way of living that is so ingrained that it can be difficult to even see its dogma at work inside us. In that, we are victims, too, even as we victimize.

The way out is getting re-sensitized—not criticized—de-socialized, and then re-socialized. If we learned it, we can unlearn it. To do that, we have to consider giving up the White male dogma, that unconscious code we're acting out. This code only props up the dangerous belief that proper White males behave in certain proper ways. I know you don't believe that. So why should you continue to support its code? Instead, I want you to support yourself, your own meaning. I want you to escape from the straitjacket, and live your life in favor of more: more you, a fully human male being.

Additionally, this book isn't about making you comfortable. Frederick Douglass said, "If there is no struggle, there is no progress. That struggle toward progress begins with truth-telling. You can do this. You can be the strong, compassionate man who takes accountability for the impact you have on society. This is a way of living—a way of *being*—with grappling as your primary way of meeting yourself and meeting the world in all its confounding complexities.

You've been trained to have to know the most, to have to have everything settled and figured out. Now you will learn to be unsettled when times are unsettling, tolerate uncertainty in uncertain times, to allow that you don't have all the answers. In this, you will find the revelations and resources of your wisest self—agile not fragile, equipped to navigate the world as it truly is, feeling more connected to yourself. Your true world awaits. Let's begin exploring!

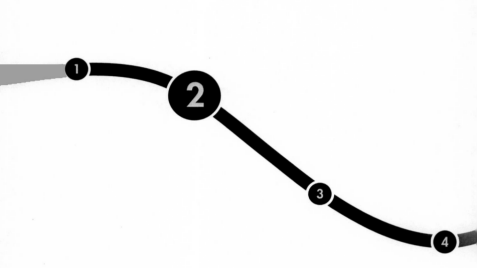

WHITE MALE SOCIALIZATION

White men grow on an open, level field. White women grow on far steeper and rougher terrain because the field wasn't made for them. Women of color grow not just on a hill, but on a cliffside over the ocean, battered by wind and waves. None of us chooses the landscape in which we're planted.
—Emily Nagoski, *The Secret to Unlocking the Stress Cycle*

Frustrating a group of White men can be easy. All you have to do is observe out loud that who they think they are is really just the sum of training. Granted, it's a training they didn't know they were involved in, but it's training nonetheless. Though each man in the group may have different names, they are all more or less a variation of a generic White person dictated by White socialization.

Most would respond with indignation, but that's because they don't understand how pervasive and invasive socialization can be.

Sociologist Charles Cooley developed an early understanding of socialization with his concept of the looking-glass self. He theorized that individuals form their identity not in solitude but in social settings and that how we are perceived plays a huge influence on our self-concept. He writes, "I am not what I think I am. I am not what you think I am. I am what I think you think I am." This is the process of socialization.

It's hard for Whites to see our socialization because we are the dominant group. Everywhere we look, we see ourselves mirrored back so that we can't see the contrast between us and others. This gives us a sense that White is the norm and everything else is the deviance. We're like the Greenwich Mean Time of race, we think.

And for White men there's even more of a world created in our own image—not by God, by other White men. We see ourselves as presidents, as pictures on currency, as movie heroes defeating the bad guy who is often easily distinguishable because he's other than a White man. We are swimming in White socialization like fish who do not know they're breathing water. Part of what keeps it in place is its invisibility to us. And we don't want to get out. And why would we when society flatters us everywhere and enables our belief in our own exceptionality? And besides, what else is there but this "normal"?

We are swimming in White socialization like fish who do not know they're breathing water. Part of what keeps it in place is its invisibility to us.

Well, reality. The real you, stifling underneath all those layers of conditioning. A great you, a larger you, a deeper you, a richer you. You can live that way, more authentically and more happily, but first you have to accept that you have been socialized and given a constructed identity. Like Jason Bourne, you are living out an agenda you did not choose.

It can be hard to accept because it's so hard to see, but it's the first piece of grappling you must do. If you feel defensive about how much of you is actually socialization disguised as you, that's a good place to start. That defensiveness is a symptom of the fragility most White people develop as a result of being part of the dominant group. It rears up because our culture preaches rugged individualism and self-determination and lets us tell ourselves we are independent of socialization. In fact, you have been deeply shaped by socialization. To acknowledge it is to begin to start to separate your real self from your socialized identity.

All people outside the dominant culture reigning in the West have an advantage when it comes to this grappling. Not being in the dominant group, they can clearly see and understand socialization at work. It allows them to question norms, especially nonsensible norms, and to think critically. It gives them a better chance to respond by choice instead of by conditioned response. They are not blind and deaf to our White and male socialization the way we are.

Imagine you are Black or brown in this country and most of the images of power you see are White. Most of the images of wealth are White. Most of the images of beauty are White. Because you are not White, you know this message is mostly *for* Whites: "Here's how to look, here's your future job, here's your future house." To us it looks "normal"—it is us being mirrored back to us. We don't question it. But everyone else sees the contrast to themselves and recognizes this as White socialization in progress, training Whites to expect certain things and behave in certain ways. Training Whites to expect privilege.

After the attacks by a largely White crowd on the Capitol building, LeBron James wrote, "We live in two Americas." The White America is the one where horses and rubber bullets and tear gas don't greet them—even when they get violent—as they do crowds protesting on behalf of Black rights. While Blacks have had to endure and grapple with what W. E. B. DuBois called a "double consciousness"—that of being Black in a White world—Whites have never had that struggle. Whites' single consciousness has left us weaker, fragile. It's flattened our ability to see things as they are, to see multidimensionally.

SOCIALIZATION

Socialization is a shared system of meaning. In fact, "much of what we call personality is not a fixed set of traits, only coping mechanisms a person acquired in childhood," writes addiction expert Dr. Gabor Maté. The impact can be that we White males tend to think our set of meanings is the only right one. For instance, when people say "the American way," they often mean the "White American way." But if you were to point that out to a fellow White male, he'd likely react defensively or at least with discomfort, as if you were forcing race into it. But think of the "American way" portrayed on TV: cornfields with a White farmer on a tractor, Friday night lights with a White quarterback, a White soldier coming home to embrace a child who runs up to meet him, a pickup truck kicking up dust as it approaches a country house where an older White couple awaits a fond reunion with family. We can all picture that.

As a fixture in our lives, TV is a powerful socialization machine. All media helps to socialize us. In fact, everything around us socializes us into our White identity, an identity that substitutes the generic for the particularity of us. Our families, schools, religious institutions, community organizations, corporations, even our government—they all socialize us, as their leaders were also socialized. We're molded to be "acceptable" in order to achieve belonging to the dominant group. And belonging has rewards. Important rewards. In this way, socialization is a sort of contract. It's the safety of predictability. You act a certain way, do certain things, and you will be rewarded within the group. But what about everyone else?

Unchallenged groupthink can be dangerous—to ourselves, to others, and to society, especially democratic society. So much of our socialized identities are unconscious already and difficult to get at without adding groupthink to the mix. Though some socialization is visible—food, dress, language—it's the tip of an iceberg, and we're unaware of the frozen mass beneath in the water. To us, it's just the world; we know it, and it makes us feel safe. Until it doesn't.

ENTITLED

Reality doesn't take a break while we are living in our cocooned worlds. No matter how we try to gate ourselves, we share the world with others, and they are not in the business of trying to help us filter out non-White, non-male views. Invariably, we witness things in our daily lives or by way of the news that make us uncomfortable. We "remember" that non-Whites exist, and in sizeable numbers, and that they feel alien. We are so socialized into Whiteness that human-ness itself in its many beautiful variations feels strange.

We have been whitewashed so much that the concepts of race and culture—well, those are for others: Black and brown people. We have been whitewashed so much that the burdens of those outside our group feel like burdens they alone should shoulder. Our verbiage reflects our abdication of responsibility for some of the damage we created. We use words such as slavery instead of enslavement. But Blacks were not slaves so much as enslaved; and White men did it to them. Ahmaud Arbery's cause of death wasn't his being Black; his cause of death was White murderous racists. We talk about the American melting pot, which will absorb everyone into the dominant society of Whiteness and male power while melting away the diverse identities of every-one else. This is a strange and impossible concept called uni-versalism: no more colors, no more accents, a homogenized cleansing. Consider that when you say things like "I don't see his color, I see people" you could be engaging in univer-salism. Universalism assumes that since we are "all one," assimilating is a good thing. However, by assimilating, those who once deviated from the norm as measured by White maleness see to our comfort. And many non-Whites know all too well the cost of making White people uncomfortable.

By making our own comfort a priority, we insist on retaining our White power structure perks while resisting self-examination when we feel discomfort. Of course, we know it's unfair that women routinely feel discomfort under the eyes of disrespectful men. But that's men being men. Of course, it's not okay that minorities feel discomfort when store clerks or security guards follow them around a store. But you in particular are not the one following them around. By washing our hands of the problems of a society built on White male privilege, we choose White over human. Our socialized beings dehumanize us.

It's important to remember, though, and an important aspect to grappling, that you've been trained to feel this way. You've been conditioned to believe you are inclined towards, even entitled to comfort, not discomfort, and to certainty, not uncertainty. But comfort and certainty don't equip you to grapple with the world as it truly is, the world where people who look like you and act like you can cross over into terrible acts. The world that pricks your conscience but defies quick solutions. The one you want to hide from in favor of the familiar world of White maleness so that you can feel comfortable again, certain again of what you're supposed to do with your days and your life. In that privileged life, we're not only entitled to comfort and certainty but also safety, opportunity, and power.

Unfortunately, all that privilege has side effects, a major one being fragility. Though we know what rules to follow in the dominant culture, we're often clueless everywhere else. We don't know how to handle ourselves and we don't know how to handle that fact. We fear it—we want to remain in our familiar waters—we demand it because otherwise we're just fish out of water, flopping on some foreign shore. We don't have the strength we need to meet the world on its terms, not our terms. In a way, our privilege has made us lazy, shallow, superficial, and unprepared for the larger world. Socialization has shaped us to avoid grappling, to avoid the deep end of things, to compete, seek the material, and call it winning, and to never venture beyond the familiar.

Meanwhile, we are living in a cultural paradigm that is rapidly becoming a thing of the past. And we have no clue where that leaves us. If you don't want to be left behind, if you don't want to feel irrelevant, just another generic White guy living out his White guy life script, you need to learn more about the socialized you that's been living your life instead of the real you.

THE WHITE WORLD VIEW

Socialization starts early, from the cradle. As Dr. Erin N. Winkler reports in her *PACE* piece "Children Are Not Colorblind: How Young Children Learn Race," studies have found that babies recognize race, and that preschoolers not only show racial bias but use race as a basis for power and inclusion or exclusion. This happened to you, too, before you even knew what was happening. Remember the television images I mentioned earlier? Children see those, too. They see male presidents and mostly male principals. They see White male pictures on money, usually male spiritual leaders heading up their churches, they see White men moving with confidence through a world that welcomes them in a way Black men are not. White is where it's at. Even Jesus is somehow White.

Now as a grownup, you are part of a system where Whiteness as a socialized construct means an assumption of superiority. Manifest Destiny, the Trail of Tears, colonialism, mass incarceration—the permission Whiteness gave—and still gives—to brutalize others looks less like superiority and more like a kind of barbarism.

Cultural appropriation speaks to more White entitlement. Think of the White-owned corporate restaurants selling "Mexican" food. They're making a mint. Remember when Donald Trump posed with a taco bowl made at the Trump Tower Grill, using it as a prop on Cinco de Mayo to exclaim, "I love Hispanics"? We can be tone-deaf to the deeper meanings of culture.

Socialized Whiteness also has us assigning identity to others. It means we end up walking in a racialized world

emotional fragility —that's it!

with a disowned but quite potent, racial identity. Minorities who don't fit a stereotype are often met with incredulity: You don't look like an *x, y, z* (too dark or too light, too tall or too short, wrong eye color). You're too articulate to be an *x, y, z* (no accent, wide vocabulary). You're an exception to *x, y, z* (successful, honest, educated, employed, a skillful driver—take your pick of the good, therefore White, trait that makes the exception to the rule).

Why do we do this? Who do we think we are? Often unintentionally, we have tried to become the arbiters of reality for everyone else. We spin reality to suit ourselves because we are fragile due to the undeveloped and underdeveloped parts of ourselves. It might be hard to identify yourself as that word: fragile. But if you can't handle your truth emotionally because it calls your certainty about the world into question, you're not going to let reality inside. You're going to use some intellectual spin to numb out any emotional reactions you might feel in your body. You'll explain it away to protect your White world view. That defensiveness, that rigidity in your emotional world to what is happening in the world around you and inside of you allows emotional fragility to flourish.

Though this seems strange—not just that we do it, but that we let ourselves get away with it—it's facilitated by our programming. Deep down we have an implicit bias toward people who look like us, White and male, and away

29

from others. And we seem to be supported in this by all the successful Whiteness being mirrored back to us. Look at all those White captains of industry, politicians, astronauts, explorers, movie stars—all that success! We White guys are amazing! And we attribute it to our hard work. We deserve that success because we have worked hard. We think we're living in a meritocracy, when actually we are living in a mirror-tocracy. White male dominance perpetuates White male dominance.

What if, when confronted by a challenge to one of our stereotypes, we didn't turn it around and start questioning someone's identity? What if when we felt defensiveness goading us to push back or become patronizing, we recognized it as a less developed part of ourselves? What if we let ourselves feel discomfort instead of fighting for comfort? What if we looked at the seeming paradox of the reality of the person in front of us and the person they're "supposed" to be to fit our world, and then went towards that discomfort inside of us rather than away?

If we grapple in that moment and let the world teach us, broadening our experience and understanding of the world, we'd be better equipped to handle ourselves in the future. We'd be more agile the next time we found ourselves confronted by something outside our experience, or even outside of our control. If we did that enough, we'd start to want to step outside our comfort zones. We'd begin to get comfortable moving beyond our conditioned identities, too.

Many of us feel shame and guilt around the privilege we've inherited, especially knowing that others have been disinherited. Your compassion for others is not misplaced, but your shame and guilt are. You haven't been taught how *right!* to be with shame and guilt, and so it remains a stuck part inside of you. And just as you might project an identity on non-Whites, society has projected one on you. Knowing that, you deserve to practice self-compassion and understanding. That kindness directed towards yourself will further increase your capacity to learn and grow. And it will present you an even starker choice: about whether to perpetuate your learned White identity or begin to unlearn it.

Male Socialization

You'll also have to start separating your actual maleness with your socialized maleness. Does this sound familiar:

- Feelings are more for women than for men; feelings make women irrational.
- Men are more naturally leaders than women.
- Competition is in men's DNA.
- Fighting and winning shows masculinity.
- I am here to make my mark by changing the world in some way, remaking it according to my own vision.
- I influence others; others don't influence me.

- Men are decisive compared to women.
- I am what I do.
- The order of my life is Do-Have-Be: I *do* things to get money. Money helps me to *have* things, and then finally I can *be* happy.

These are all conditioned beliefs about maleness. Let's look at a few, starting with feelings. Feelings are for all people, and I have never heard of a woman punching a hole in her own wall that she will later have to patch because she is in the grip of irrational emotion. Anger has often been the one emotion men feel comfortable expressing.

We tend to assume men are better leaders because we have been exposed to a world of them. Remember, we are not living in a meritocracy but a mirror-tocracy.

If men are what they do, it means their existence is not rooted in being—in being a human being.

And men's supposed resistance to influence? First, that's about holding on to power, going back to that notion of dominate or be dominated. Second, it excludes chances to learn and grow even from the people we love most in the world. Husbands do this all the time.

When I first hung up my therapist shingle, I advertised myself as a couples therapist because I love the dynamic work of working with two people. In couples counseling, there are three types of connection. You can turn away,

Couples work

turn toward, or turn against. Couples usually come in turning away or turning against. Part of my work was helping them turn toward each other.

As I built my practice little by little, I understood that some people were choosing me partly because I am a man. The husband, the wife would say, was more comfortable with a guy because then he wouldn't feel "outnumbered." It's possible these men saw themselves in me and expected that I'd see myself in them. We were members of the "guy club" with its well-established tenets and expectations.

The wife usually came in as the complainant, expressing some desire for more of this or less of that. She'd lay out a case at the beginning about why they were there. After acknowledging her share and making sure I understood, I'd ask the husband about his response to her request or complaint. And usually he'd make some defensive move: She's exaggerating. That's not actually what happened. She's making a big deal of something. She's irrational.

This happens a lot with couples, the husband not grappling. What I found in my cases is that he doesn't actually want change. When she does, rather than deal with the complaint, the reason she wanted change—he would bring up another issue where *she* was at fault. He wouldn't bring up this counter-complaint because he wanted to create change. He'd bring it up to deflect. He'd hold on to it, waiting until the wife brought up her issue. And then at that somewhat consciously chosen moment, he'd pull it out of his back pocket and say, "Well, you know what? You do this." But the net effect of this on therapy and transformation in the marriage is that it grinds down dialogue, bringing change and growth to a halt. And the result would be what he consciously or unconsciously wanted all along—keep the status quo.

A man doing this doesn't actually want to hear what she has to say. What they really want is for her to get off his case: "She's on my back a lot. She's constantly criticizing me. I can't do anything. I'm walking on eggshells." And, although this might be true, what's more generally true is that the husbands are using their complaints to shield themselves from what their wives want. It keeps the spouses in separate camps where the husbands don't have to be influenced or changed by their wives. In fact, the husbands perceived these efforts toward influence and change as a kind of threat and changing a kind of weakness. While the wives did the work of turning towards, the husbands kept turning away or turning against.

ha!

I grew so frustrated with dudes. I would be like, come on, buddy. She's just asking for this *x* thing. It's not the moon. You can do it.

Early on, I trained with Dr. John Gottman, who teaches research-based methods. Dr. Gottman, after working with thousands of couples, made the unequivocal statement that men need to be open to being influenced by their wives. They need to be open to the change their wife and their marriage is offering them. Though men may not emote in the same way, they can learn to connect in their relationships. They can learn to be emotionally present. They can learn to stop turning away.

So why don't they? *million dollar Question!*

Open to influence is not part of the guy club code. We're White men, on top of the social hierarchy. It's *our* place to do the influencing and dominating. For us, adaptation and change are optional. If I were to share with other men that my wife is really teaching me about patience by helping me become more vulnerable to my emotions and more vulnerable to emotional intimacy, I'd be dismissed from the guy club.

What does that say about us—this notion that being influenced by a woman (*the woman we love!*) is laughable? It says that along with having racial bias, we also have sexist patterns we learned from society. Whether we choose to stay that way going forward is our choice.

SEEING IS BELIEVING *Absolutely*

But we can't change what we don't see in ourselves. Many of us don't even really believe we still have a paternalistic society. Even in the age of #MeToo, a lot of us tend to think of these terrible stories of women suffering at the hands of men as exceptions. It's the "bad apple" theory again, the same one used to deny systemic racism in police departments across the country.

But if sexism isn't commonplace with real-world consequences to women, then why do they still make less than us men for the same jobs? They earn more college degrees than we do; why isn't that reflected in the job market? If women as "less than" isn't ingrained in our culture, how come women still get blamed for "what they were wearing" or "how much they had to drink"? If women are valued and respected, why is the average number of sexual attacks against women about 250,000 annually, according to RAINN? If we don't have a sexist society run by sexist men, why do women candidates get judged for being too ambitious while their male counterparts are lauded for the same? Would you trust a woman to repair your car? If not, why not?

Instead of putting so much energy into resisting sexism as a damaging and widespread phenomenon in general, it's better to assume that you as a White male, given your socialization, have learned socialized patterns of sexism. Don't waste time getting defensive or resisting the feelings of shame. Be on the lookout for the telltale signs of your social conditioning. It doesn't mean you're a bad person, it means you've been socialized in very normal ways. Many therapists strive to help their clients understand the role of unconscious actions and conditioning. Just because we aren't aware of it doesn't mean it isn't true.

I know when a lot of my own conditioning occurred. I went to an all-male boarding school for high school. I have a PhD in the guy code. It includes the misogynistic "bros before hos" comradery; the belief that feelings are for sissies unless it's to occasionally lash out in anger; that we are supposed to go a-conquering and hopefully have a sexual conquest; and prove through competition that we are winners, not losers. It also included disdaining further learning and emphasizing what we already know; and resisting being accountable to a woman because you'll be on a leash that later turns to a ball and chain when you marry. When we participate in the code even in part, we reinforce it to ourselves and to the other guys around us. We perpetuate it, and we police each other to keep it going. The code owns us and warps what masculinity means for each of us before we can even get a chance to grow into ourselves.

Anyone who watched Brett Kavanaugh's 2018 Supreme Court confirmation hearings saw that in action. The whole hearing made it clear Kavanaugh was a guy-code guy even in high school. And here's this educated, vulnerable, intelligent woman staring at almost all White male faces who then refuse to grapple with this obvious sexist situation, this horrible assault situation. Kavanaugh starts lashing out, speaking about beer and yearbooks, his outburst a backlash against being held accountable. This contrasted to the woman saying he'd assaulted her, a woman who had continued to grow and had become an accomplished adult. But the White men listening to the testimony confirmed Kavanaugh on to the court anyway. And now Kavanaugh is on the court, where issues involving women will come before him. How will he preside over cases involving the intimate and deeply personal nature of womanhood? Will his decisions change the power dynamic men hold over women in this country? It is a study in the perpetuation of White male power.

THE WAR ON BOYS' FEELINGS

How many times were you told not to cry as a child? To be a man? To not be "butt-hurt." To suck it up, to deal with it? How many times were you conditioned to see your heart, the expression of it as a dangerous agitator who might have you labeled as some sort of faulty male? How many times did you revert to emotional stoicism?

Yet, as author Glennon Doyle points out in her book *Untamed,* "Human qualities are not gendered. What is gendered is permission to express certain traits." In our culture, we males are not allowed to feel a full range of emotion. So trained are we that many men can't even identify what they feel beyond the labels of good or bad.

WHITE MALE SOCIALIZATION

Naturally, we often believe anything that makes us feel bad is something bad in itself, whether that's protests on television, the disappointment of your wife, or the sales clerk who doesn't notice us. As men, we feel entitled to comfort, especially emotional comfort. Because we "deserve" to be comfortable, in our relationships with women we tend not to want to come to terms with their feelings and their issues, while expecting them to be accountable to ours. Again, this is programming, learned patterns. But it doesn't change the fact that men can be *emotional gold diggers*. Because we reject our feelings, untrained in how to navigate them in the first place, we unconsciously expect women to hold our feelings for us. They are supposed to endlessly understand, read our hearts and read our minds, to be patient with our feelings, to feel compassion and tenderness and take care of us.

As if they are our mothers instead of our partners. As if we are their children. They do the work in the relationship while we unconsciously abdicate responsibility for ourselves. They are expected to do our emotional labor for us.

Making the one-sided situation worse is this ingrained notion in our American history labeled "rugged individualism" by President Herbert Hoover. Instead of learning belongingness and intimacy, of give and take and reciprocity, we learn that we should try to need no one and to go it alone, as if preparing to go off on a wilderness trek

solar hero

and wrestle wild bears. The only bear that needs wrestling with is the one that lives inside of us, resisting the change needed to stay relevant in a changing world.

If one good thing can be said about male socialization, it is that we speak its language and act it out so obviously, that it gives us a chance to see it more clearly than our racial biases. Not all of us could be jocks after all or the best at being sarcastic. We lived according to comparisons of ourselves to ourselves, which does let us see the code we used as measurement. Going off script may make you anxious: what is a male if not described by the code?

A male is you, whomever you turn out to be when you actually act from inside your own sense of meaning.

Years ago, I had an athletic injury that required a physical therapist to work through and break up scar tissue. It was a painful process to have him massage the scar tissue until it was all gone. This painful repair is a perfect metaphor for the process of undoing our White male socialization. You'll need to take it slow, be kind to yourself, and not worry that on the other side of socialization it may feel like you will be alone. Socialization can warp you but not permanently. You may have contorted yourself to try to fit into societal norms, but the un-contorted you will feel more natural in the end. It's liberation and the end of a lot of pain that has limited your mobility. It's the beginning of a lot of joy.

(handwritten margin note: uncontorting from socialization)

WHITE MALE SOCIALIZATION
How Conformity Leads to Inauthenticity

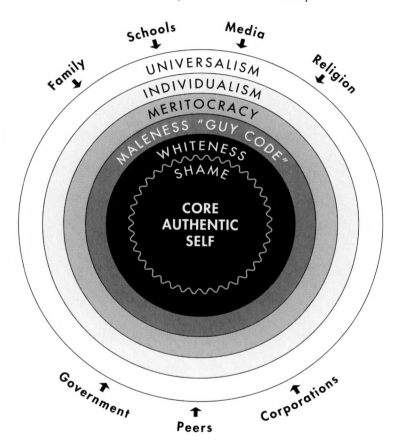

Socialization builds its many layers around our true core, leaving us far out of touch with ourselves, experiencing life through filters of socialized behavior and shame.

Empathy will undergird some of that joy. Socialization costs men in empathy. It stymies bonding, not just with others but with the pieces of our fragmented selves. All those orphaned parts of you, shunned by heartless socialization—empathy unites them so we can show up as our whole selves. And then in turn, we can unite the pieces of our external world, to bond to it and thereby belong to it. With empathy, we bring back together the exiled parts of ourselves, notice the parts that are trying to protect us, turn outward to connect with others, and find the gentle places where we belong.

Grappling is your route to reclaiming your whole self. The White male narrative scripted the past, has scripted the present, and is plotting the script for the future. Because of this, both collectively and individually men's internal worlds have kept the world stuck. But grappling rewrites the past, empowers the present, and re-envisions the future—your future. By reclaiming yourself, one piece at a time, you help reclaim the world for all beings, shifting it towards a better lived present and future.

how would you teach empathy
to a Man?

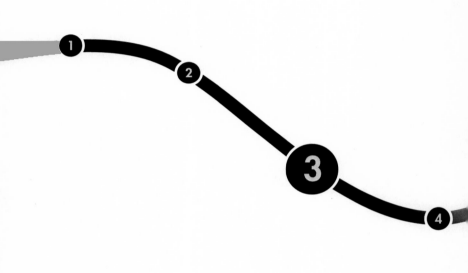

THE COST OF NOT GRAPPLING
DANGEROUS FRAGILITY

"I sit on a man's back, choking him and making him carry me, and yet assure myself and others that I am very sorry for him and wish to ease his lot by all possible means—except by getting off his back."
—Leo Tolstoy, *What Then Must We Do?*

In the West, we men have inherited a lot of "original sin." Of course, there's the original sin of racism. It glares out from the Declaration of Independence like a fly caught in amber. The U.S. Constitution also showcases slavery in the three-fifth's compromise found in Article I, Section 2, which got down to the business of calculating how many members states could send to the U.S. House of Representatives: "Representatives and direct Taxes shall be apportioned among the several States which may be included within this Union, according to their respective Numbers, which shall be determined by adding to the whole Number of free Persons, including those bound to Service for a Term of Years, and excluding Indians not taxed, three-fifths of all other Persons."

We've never overcome our original sin; from the beginning of the country to this day, laws have either been passed that perpetuate systemic racism or, maybe more tellingly, laws have not been passed to overturn systemic racism.

The original sin of sexism has an even longer history, and here, too, we tolerate it. In our Judeo-Christian White man world, we have Eve dependent on Adam for her very existence. It's a strange inversion, since in the real world, women and men both rely on women's bodies to make their entrance into life. But the tale has worked as part of a propaganda of subservience and subjugation that insists men are meant to be dominant. The Adam and Eve tale justifies this subjugation by laying all the blame for expulsion from Eden at Eve's feet. She can't be trusted. Better put it in men's hands, this building of civilizations and governance and religion. In the United States, women didn't get the right to vote until 1920. If Eve's judgment couldn't be trusted, though, how could Adam's be? He ate the apple, too. She grappled with the Father of Lies. Where was Adam? Eve shouldered the blame for the both of them.

When you look at how long these ideas of racism and sexism have persisted, it's more accurate to say these "original sins" are *ongoing* sins. They persist because those in power, we White men, refuse to grapple with them. And so, the harm continues.

Anytime there is a refusal to grapple, harm follows. That "refusal" doesn't have to be conscious for it to qualify as refusal. Maintaining silence, claiming ignorance is refusal. So is using our position of power to exempt us from grappling with questions about power and race, dominance and gender. We must consciously, *willingly* seek to identify and understand the suffering that not grappling in the past has caused our society. In reality, we won't have to strain too much to see all the harm our refusal to grapple in the present is causing.

Demographic and societal changes have resulted in racial progress for Black and brown people, as well as for women. Years ago, racism and sexism were real and overt. Until 1974, for instance, women didn't have the legal right to get credit cards in their own names. In the sixties, women couldn't attend Ivy League schools. No getting into military schools such as West Point either. And control of her own body? Blurry boundaries at best. Certainly, there's been progress.

And we've seen true racial progress made, too. In World War II, troops were segregated. Fast forward to a Black Commander-in-Chief in Barack Obama. And 2020 saw the first Black and Asian woman elected to Vice President.

But progress has been halting. In 1870, the first Black U.S. senator, Hiram Revels took office filling seats vacant since Mississippi seceded, including a seat held by Confederate Jefferson Davis. So why, since then, have only ten Black U.S. senators served?

The first female senator Rebecca Felton started serving in 1922. In 2021, fifty-four women have served—in history. Why do so few serve now? (In 2021, only twenty-four serve out of one hundred.) Because the forces of socialization push back.

Though we've seen racial progress, we've simultaneously seen an enormous amount of *racist* progress. In the Trump era, overt displays of racism became far more common. None of us will soon forget the parade of young White men carrying tiki torches through the night, brazenly marching to the chant, "Jews will not replace us!" Nor will we forget the storming of the U.S. Congress by a pro-Trump crowd that included racist hate groups that wanted to overturn a national election to create anarchy. Or because they view the Right as being more hospitable toward their racism.

And then we had to witness many elected Republican politicians seeming to prove them right.

It may be tempting to believe that mainstream Americans harbor none of the extreme prejudices we've seen expressing themselves during Trump's term. But we've seen too many images of Whites confronting non-Whites and people with accents to demand they justify their presence in a campus common area, a bird-watching area, their own front yards, at stoplights—"Karen" or "Ken" videos multiplied on social media.

Racism and sexism hadn't gone away: they had just become more subtle and nuanced, inflicted indirectly by way of microaggressions and racially tinged jokes or corporate boards comprised of entirely White men. And then came the Trump era, where overt bigotry could rear up its ugly, violent head.

It can come as a shock, these overt displays, and we usually don't know what to do when it happens right in front of us. Many of us just want to get the hell out of there, away from the scene. Though it's great that we want to disassociate ourselves from racism, bailing on a scene doesn't combat it, either. We may not be racist, but we're also not anti-racist, as historian Imbram X. Kendi noted in his 2019 book *How to Be an Antiracist*. But we must.

It can be hard to see racism in systems. Whites have tended to see it in individuals instead of societal collectives of peoples. And, looking at oneself, we tend to think, "If I'm a good person, I can't also be racist. That false dichotomy acts to perpetuate racism. We also have to challenge ourselves to see it in our systems: our government, our corporations, our schools. It's harder to do so but an important part of being an anti-racist in today's world. To just not be an abuser rather than actively anti-abuser is to be a passive abuser at worst and complicit at best.

We may be uncomfortable with overt racist displays, but we're also uncomfortable with the notion of taking a stand, helping to upend certain parts of our society right now. Uncomfortable looking into our own unconscious racism learned from a larger society that is racist at a foundational, systemic level. The discomfort stems, in part, from this notion that we must give something up, lose something if power is distributed equitably. Where do we end up if our world is turned over? On the bottom?

FRAGILITY'S LOSE-LOSE STATUS QUO PROPOSITION

Probably not on the bottom, but your fragility likely won't believe me when I tell you that. Because so much of what it means to be a White man is built on power *over* others, we are deeply dependent on the notion of a power hierarchy to know who we are. It's our identity orientation: over, not under.

THE COST OF NOT GRAPPLING

This is part of how fragility grows. When someone does have power over us, especially someone outside our privileged group, it triggers "bad" feelings. We feel frustrated, angry, maybe humiliated without reason. We defend, minimize, push back, argue, ignore, or withdraw. All these actions are really reactions to our construct being challenged, and they act to restore a kind of equilibrium to how we see the world. We want to flip the dynamic, we want to somehow overpower the one who has power over us. Otherwise, we're in an untenable situation. We've got to return it to our comfortable, familiar status quo. A status quo that justifies what I next do to you because of what you did, or even might do, to me.

But think about what that means. The fragile part of you is fighting instances of power distribution in real life. It won't tolerate diversity in power situations. You don't consider yourself a racist or a sexist, so why does the idea of power sharing feel so—*wrong*?

Because it does not mirror you. Remember, you've been conditioned to have biased views, even sexist and racist views. In certain ways, such covert bigotry is more dangerous than overt racial slurs. Covert bigotry means deniability. You can deny it even to yourself. Imagine the power such a covert force wields when we can't even identify it, let alone even see it.

This denial leads to another cost of not grappling: we White men often can't acknowledge the damage we're doing, even to ourselves. In his book *Dying of Whiteness: How the Politics of Racial Resentment Is Killing America's Heartland*, physician Jonathan M. Metzl studies the ways in which White Americans' embrace of conservative politicians and policies have hurt voters. The policies were supposedly designed to boost White voters' quality of life in the heartland. Cuts to social services and schools, and pro-gun and anti-Affordable Care Act attitudes didn't lead to some new day of White prosperity, though. While hurting women, children, and minorities, conservative efforts likewise hurt Whites. The cost to these White voters included increased suicide by gun, increased school dropouts, and lessening life expectancies, according to Metzl. White voters' refusal to grapple with today's America in favor of recapturing White America's past "greatness" creates a lose–lose for all citizens. Yet, many continue to support those who keep promising a ticket to the past via right-leaning policies. To them, it's better not to grapple with harmful White socialized identities—better to keep an image of themselves from an earlier era—even when it goes against their own self-interest.

And in not grappling, we reinforce our fragility and our socialization. When challenged on it, we don't react well. Instead, we tend to reflexively defend ourselves. When something makes us upset—say, images of buildings burning—we don't try to understand context or challenge our kneejerk emotional reaction, usually against protesters out at night (we've also been conditioned to value property, even over life). And if we feel uneasy at our own biased stirrings, we shove any negative feelings into a Pandora's box of shame we keep stored between our hearts (our core selves) and the world. And we don't dare open that. We do not reflect, learn, and grow. We do not grapple. We remain unable and unwilling to actually wade into the mysterious and turbulent waters of our modern world.

STUCK IN THE STATUS QUO

Unfortunately, the changing world doesn't want to stay stuck in the past with us. If we White men stay comfortable and dry on our own little islands as though only we count, some unavoidable change will come along to toss us into deep water and there we'll be, unable to swim.

Part of our privilege is that thinking that our own island counts first and foremost, only to be altered by we ourselves. We aren't always asked to consider the effects of what we do on anyone or anything else. We develop this attitude by way of the socialized value of rugged individualism and of somehow earning it based on our hard work. A telling illustration is found in the deadly COVID-19 pandemic. Why was it so difficult to sell the American public on wearing masks—masks that prevent death and disease? The shared sacrifice necessary for the "common good" of limiting the spread of a pandemic became a difficult sell to certain parts of the American citizenry. "You can't tell me what to do! I have free will. This is about liberty!" Meanwhile, our Canadian neighbors got their pandemic under control, readily wearing masks because of their ingrained sense of communal responsibility.

Wearing masks became something too different, outside the status quo, something not done on our islands. Many would not adapt—could not adapt because they struggled to manage their own discomfort at the change in behavior that mask wearing, for example, asked of us. We paid the cost in lives and lost health, in recession and livelihoods erased. A social catastrophe—that was the cost of not grappling, all to stay stuck in old ways of thinking and doing.

As White males, we are particularly responsible, because so many of us hold the power in America. In *Winners Take All: The Elite Charade of Changing the World*, author Anand Giridharadas writes about how the role of government used to be to create change, particularly during the social programs of the sixties and seventies. But over time, the onus to create change has shifted to the marketplace, to wealthy businessmen. As the income gap widens in our country, there's a growing resentment toward those powerful, wealthy people, who have no incentive to create real, positive change. After all, the rich are the biggest beneficiaries of the current status quo and power system.

Winners Take All details how these elite entrepreneurs—for the most part White men—give money to charitable programs, maybe even create their own foundations, and they want this work to be a feel-good, win–win change. The problem is that this charitable giving does not solve the larger system of inequity. It addresses the *victims* of an unfair system, but it never addresses the *perpetrators*. It does not shift the balance of power. It's window dressing, bandaging wounds, while the real harm to society continues to spiral. White male corporate leadership may invest in change supporting those less fortunate, but when it comes to addressing the larger systemic issues that live in our culture and our institutions, the interest in change wanes.

There's a disconnection there, a failure of understanding and imagination. For example, the book details how psychologist Amy Cuddy speaks to largely male corporate boards and large investor meetings. As a speaker, Cuddy knows the value of connecting with an audience through story. As she tries to lay out her point about the difficulty women have in corporations and the huge loss for the companies in their lack of gender diversity, she first makes the connection for the CEOs to their daughters. They get it as they call to mind the wives and daughters they know in their lives. But as she tries to apply it to women in general, women as a group of people, she can sense she is losing the room. The associative thinking needed to connect the dots between the daughter at home and women in society is missing. Lost is the ability to see the interconnectedness between things.

But our brains weren't designed to learn things in isolation; we group things together naturally. But socialization can atrophy that ability as we refuse to see things in the larger patterns that they fundamentally exist within. Growth falters when we no longer use our associative learning ability to see things in greater context. Such learning is important to grappling, to seeing what is really there, not just what we have been conditioned to see.

Meanwhile, back in the heartland, folks keep behaving in the ways Jonathan Metzl laid out in *Dying of Whiteness*. Traveling across the heartland, the psychiatry and sociology professor consistently found that anxiety about race led to negative impacts. Whites who were anxious and fearful about changing racial demographics cast themselves as the victims, decided they needed guns to protect themselves, and voted to repeal gun-control laws. The same people resisted President Obama's Affordable Care Act, even though it helped so many of the working poor that made up their towns. Without even realizing it, White people acted as their own worst enemies.

That has led, as Ijeoma Oluo observed in *Mediocre: The Dangerous Legacy of White Male America*, to a kind of systemic mediocracy. It's a mediocre life for ourselves, and for the people and society around us. She writes, "While we

what motivates a way to do some "intense emotional labor"??

THE COST OF NOT GRAPPLING

would like to believe otherwise, it is usually not the cream that rises to the top; our society rewards behaviors that are actually disadvantageous to everyone. Studies have shown that the traits long considered signs of strong leadership (like overconfidence and aggression) are in reality disastrous in both business and politics."

Grappling won't give us control over this legacy. But it will help us look at the past in a new light, getting us past the old tropes that have so damaged our society. And it will help us empower the present and re-envision a future in which we are working toward our collective good. It will help pull us out of the status quo rut. It will help us feel less helpless and less victimized.

GRAPPLING ISN'T EASY, BUT IT'S THE BETTER BET

Challenging the assumptions of the past means intense emotional labor. It is much harder than just accepting the narrative we've been handed, the system of domination that we've internalized and see every day. But this challenge, this internal questioning, is necessary. From weakness comes strength. From fragile, we go to agile. The hard work eventually becomes easier as we build the wrestling muscle by asking ourselves tough questions about how we got here and what our next steps forward are.

How to begin to grapple (handwritten)

Questioning our identity and socialization will feel strange and uncomfortable. We've never been forced to confront the killing of Native Americans, the enslavement of Africans, the subjugation of women—especially in ways that are personal and emotional instead of just an intellectual exercise. Yet the legacies of our past are all around us every day, part of the White privilege status quo, the one that caters to our convenience and comfort. In fact, we become unwitting agents of the status quo when we refuse to grapple. Why would any of us hard-working and decent men willingly choose to be part of the modern-day oppression machine? We wouldn't. And so we must grapple.

Do (handwritten)

A fundamental piece of grappling is separating ourselves from the problems and biases we inherited. We can be both a good person and subject to unconsciously internalized racist and sexist messages. If I feel as if difficult conversations, books, articles, or social media posts pose a challenge to my character, then I'll staunchly defend myself. But if I can instead see that every day, I am taking in sub-optimal messages about myself and the world around me, and then start to think critically about them, I'll be less inclined to react. Instead of being touchy in difficult situations, I can engage with a roll-up-the-sleeves attitude knowing that a hard conversation is not personal, and that I have a responsibility to be open to my history and the history of my country. Grappling leads to less conflict.

A well-known model of social interaction, Karpman's drama triangle, says that every conflict features three roles: the villain (or perpetrator), the victim, and the hero. *Drama Triangle* We may not want to think of ourselves as a victim, but I'm betting it wouldn't take you long to recall more than a few scenes of you, your male friends, and our public male examples shouldering that victim role as if born to it. How many times have you heard about tokenism costing men a job, about a crazy ex that ruined a good life, about any manner of problems being the fault of someone else? We men do it a lot, and this can often give us permission to act aggressively from a place of grievance.

If we're the victims, we have to cast a perpetrator. When women or Black or Indigenous People of Color (BIPOC) challenge our sense of comfort, our worldview, our sense that convenience is our right, we've found our villains. If, for example, we struggle to accept the real and normal reactions of Black people angry at the injustices perpetrated against them, we are simultaneously resisting seeing them as victims of an ongoing systemic racism founded 400 years ago in slavery. What we see instead is we ourselves being subjected to their unjust anger. And so we attack, feeling that it's our right to defend ourselves against a perpetrator, and we look for heroes such as politicians who speak to our own sense of victimization and say they'll elevate us. This is the drama triangle at work.

grappling And here's where grappling is hard. Instead of attacking others, we have to engage in close combat *with ourselves*. If we are victims, we are, too, the perpetrators. And we can be the hero, as well. We have to look at ourselves in all three roles to really understand the role we're taking up in any given situation. If you refuse to grapple this way, you pay for it by playing the victim over and over throughout your life.

And, meanwhile, we keep lashing out at the so-called perpetrators, which can lead to dark results. Take that iconic 2020 image, the St. Louis couple pointing guns at protestors outside their home. That's fear, fear that "those people" are going to take over and come for us. Such fear generated rumors of people out for violence, hiding there in crowds of largely peaceful protesters marching for racial justice. Which they have the right to do. They were not the perpetrators, but they were cast that way. And who became the hero? To those casting themselves as the victims of protester "mobs," it became an armed couple brandishing weapons at people validly and peacefully exercising civil rights. The drama triangle becomes a repetitive "story" playing out against one another over and over again. There is no new narrative, no new oxygen to rewrite the story.

It's important to grapple with difficult questions and issues, no matter how ill at ease you are, because those who refuse often begin to panic about "those people" disrupting their way of life. Soon, "those people" are so threatening and dangerous that we dehumanize them. Sociologists have noted this phenomenon of dehumanization in our language with one another. It has been on the rise as our socializations insist on having their own way. When we see the "other" as somehow sub-human, we can do and say anything about them. Certain more extreme people can take this so far they justify ending lives. And then someone goes through with it, shooting up a mall or a synagogue or a gay nightclub. Fear leading to violence is one of the high costs of not grappling as we White men weaponize our feelings. ✕

OTHERIZING

In a world of you, me, and them—a world that actually does take all kinds of differences to keep everything going—wouldn't you rather belong to something larger than you and all your mirror images? Wouldn't those connections of belonging serve you better than your current narrow circle? *Some may be too scared, lack of control*

If you can see the sense in that, if you are willing to stop paying the costs for your exclusive, exclusionary White man's club, you have to consider letting go of this "otherizing."

Otherizing is easy to find in the dominant culture. It's on full display during debates on unemployment benefits.

I'm sure you've heard them: "We've paid a lot in taxes to give away all these way too generous unemployment benefits. Unemployment is paying more than these people would get at their jobs. We need to get them back to work. Our taxes should stop supporting them."

Note the otherizing language. *We've* been generous. *These people* are just slackers. This is how we make "others" the primary suspects in their own demise. This is how we have become a culture of blaming the victims, turning them into the perpetrators. Without the accountability that grappling creates, we resort to saying it's *their* fault, those "other" people. They didn't work hard enough to have insurance and a nice house and pay their bills. Meanwhile, the people who created the systemic inequality in the first place get off scot-free, sometimes even glorified.

Not grappling means we don't discover the answers to the real questions: Why are so many people working so hard to make so little? How can we change this system—our system where so many are losing. Who is benefitting from inequalities in access and wealth? And are there certain advantages that we don't name to one another that go beyond the notion of merit? This work hard, "pull yourselves up by your bootstraps" narrative is quite powerful. And it's increasingly untrue. When are we willing to grapple with the stories that we as Americans continue to tell ourselves about our country and how it was founded? Do textbooks really teach the horrors of slavery including the free slave labor the American economy was built on? And if not, why not? What is it about learning the full truth about our history that feels so difficult? Perhaps we should consider that when a people struggle to grapple, the country they belong to takes on those similar qualities of not grappling and the fragility that it accompanies.

If you find yourself otherizing, take it as an invitation to grapple and reject overly simplistic narratives that reinforce your world view rather than challenge it. Consider a question about what is really happening here as a beginning. Don't look for a simple answer as a way out of not wrestling with tougher more complicated issues. People evolve, cultures evolve. Discussions must, too.

Stop labeling other people as the villains and the authors of our distress. Stop judging the person using food stamps to pay for groceries and start re-thinking the billionaires who control so much of the world's wealth. Get uncomfortable as you consider the widening gap between rich and poor, the shrinking wealth pool being divvied up among 99 percent of us. If you, as part of the White men in power, could open your heart and acknowledge the realities of the too-hard-working poor, to move them from the *other column* to the *us circle*, you've taken the first step of living more authentically with your full humanity. When we see the humanity in others we can allow it to exist in us.

And likewise, when we open to our own humanity, we can create a space for it to exist in others. Even in those who we have found most to blame for our society's ills.

Finding the moral capacity and emotional depth to acknowledge that the world is ambiguous, nuanced, complex, and challenging is uncomfortable, downright unsettling. There are no easy fixes. We may not have the power to fix anything "out there," but we can create the power to start to repair ourselves and stop paying the costs of not grappling. We can struggle with hard questions and hard choices and emerge better able to navigate an increasingly complex world.

What if that St. Louis couple had been open to grappling? What if they had turned their fear into compassion, refusing to otherize? What if they had looked at the protesters as part of their wider circle, with empathy and curiosity about what the protesters were feeling? What if they had wondered, *What's it like to be Black in our country? What needs to change? What things about me need to change so I begin doing right instead of turning away or turning against?*

It's vital to grapple this way to escape the "White insulation" Robin DiAngelo writes about in her bestselling book *White Fragility.* She points out that when we lack exposure to other ways of being, we become easily triggered when the bubble around us starts to break. Hillary Clinton's run for president was an enormous trigger, resulting in a powerful backlash from people who didn't know how to deal with such a powerful woman. Too many people lacked the skills to navigate such a break in their White male insulation. They were threatened, outraged that their comfort was disturbed. Some might even say they regressed to vote for Trump, who promised to return America to greatness (that is, a return to White is might). Aggressive voting actions and hostility and lock-her-up chants may look like power on the outside. In fact, they broadcast internal fragility. Fragility on the inside looks like rigidity on the outside.

FROM FRAGILE TO AGILE

When I walk into buildings as a White man, I can see that I'm part of the dominant group. Because I value grappling, I try to either in the moment or afterwards ask questions such as, "I wonder what it's like for women in a boardroom, where only two of the fourteen people around the table are women? Or what is it like for the one Black person in the room?"

Then, I might think about my own experiences that might help me get some insight. For instance, because I am in the therapy world, I am often one of only a few men in the room. I've grown to like that because I value the heart women bring to meetings along with their intellect. It's

prejudice + power = discrimination

certainly a different experience from what I experienced in my all-male boarding school.

I was also routinely the only White person in a setting full of Black people at my father's construction site. I'd look around and say, "This is unusual." Certainly, I was uncomfortable, but I didn't feel unsafe. My task was to just be with those feelings, knowing they would eventually metabolize into a deeper, stronger wisdom gained through the experience. I found value in it. I did not react with suspicion and a defensive kind of fear, as I could have. I didn't need to defend or find someone at fault for my discomfort.

By finding a way to relate and even empathize, I reject fragility in favor of grappling. Taking the opportunity to grapple even insulates me from automatically taking in damaging socialization messages. Instead of falling for messages telling me that marginalized people trying to push through their challenges are making trouble for us by doing it in the public eye, I realize I need to support them. Instead of feeling threatened as they succeed in breaking through traditional barriers to their own freedom and equitable treatment, I can applaud and amplify their voices and their success.

As the saying goes, "You know you have privilege when equality feels like oppression and discrimination." But discrimination can only exist when there is prejudice and power. Although Black people can certainly be prejudiced, in general, they don't have the power that is necessary to

internal dialogue

produce discrimination. And so in reality there is no "reverse discrimination." That defensive fear remains, though, and we see it play a powerful role in the wave of horrific police brutality cases. Police often use the term "reasonable fear" to defend why they drew their weapon to shoot a suspect. The problem with the "reasonable fear" argument is that so many White officers don't understand their own feelings and what they mean. They haven't grappled. They don't know how to assess their own fear, how to calmly navigate the situation. They're too fragile for that. They only know how to act. Then follows those instants when officers decide they are the victims and the suspect is the perpetrator. Instead of grappling internally, they react externally: they shoot, attack, or suffocate a suspect. To what extent are we teaching the police how to grapple with their own internal world and the particular fear that emerges in crises and life and death situations? We're not, of course. And what a cost.

Again, failure to grapple always causes harm. Not just in the world, not just to others, but to you. Your socialization causes internal injuries.

How familiar are these to you?

- There is no room for mistakes. If I'm not right, I'm wrong.
- Life is supposed to be easy and comfortable. But there's all these annoyances everywhere.

- Competition is the way of things.
- There are good feelings and bad feelings.
- A racist incident uncovers a bad apple.
- I am a doer, a go-getter.
- It's better to stick with the known and familiar.
- Seeing is believing. Show me the evidence.
- Go big or go home.
- I'm good at having answers.

At least a few of these resonated with you, didn't they? They resonate with most White men. They are outgrowths of your conditioning, harsh and stark. Consider an alternative way of seeing things:

- There is room for mistakes. If I'm not right, I get to learn and practice. Life is practice.
- Life isn't supposed to be easy and comfortable. It can be hard and uncomfortable. And I can be comfortable with discomfort, especially because it's a signal to pay attention and look for opportunities to move things.
- Competition makes you vulnerable to loss. Collaboration, on the other hand, gives you strength in numbers.
- Good feelings, bad feelings—no, all feelings are valuable and fine.

- A racist incident points to systemic racism. We are all part of that system. We can all contribute toward change and the undoing of that system.
- I am a being first. Doer can grow out of being.
- Sticking with the known and familiar is less dynamic than exploring the unknown and unfamiliar. Those beget a kind of generative growth.
- Without evidence, I have a mystery to explore.
- Without answers, I may question. Leaning into questions will help me lean into the adventure that is my life.

If we are to stop paying so much for our White privilege, if we are to move toward more fulfilling lives, we need to learn how to move beyond our socialization into someone unfamiliar but vastly superior to you as you are right now. We need to give up our dependency on fragility, resist playing out our usual roles, and regrasp our humanity.

TAKE OFF YOUR MASK

Wow! (handwritten)

Businessman and former pro football player Lewis Howes addressed a need to live authentically in his book *The Mask of Masculinity: How Men Can Embrace Vulnerability, Create Strong Relationships, and Live Their Fullest Lives.* Howes talks about how he realized at age thirty that his identity was built on misguided beliefs about what it meant to be a man. He had learned these false ideas from his teammates, coaches, stereotypes, and the media. He grew up angry, frustrated, and chasing an unknown force that left him unfulfilled.

Howes embarked on a personal journey to undo these forces and find out what it really means to be a man. He discovered that men wear masks, walls that hold back their emotion: The joker mask. The stoic mask. The athlete mask that makes them physically strong. The material mask that makes money. The sexual mask that leads them to "conquer" women. The aggressive mask that makes them see everything as competition. The invincible mask, impenetrable to any kind of struggle or weakness. The alpha mask, in which information is currency, which can lead to the infamous and annoying "mansplaining."

Men develop these masks without even realizing it. They not only show these masks to others, but to themselves, as well. Men don't realize that behind those masks lies their innate goodness, their vulnerability, their deep tenderness. They fear that if they toss out the masks, they may lose their edge, their competitiveness, and their earning capacity. Lose the masks and they might become soft.

We have to lose those masks.

If we want to be the hero of our own stories, more than just a minor character in some masculine story written

Go Inwards, lose the distractions

long ago—if *you* want to be your own hero, you must find your own strengths and your own helpers who can equip you for battle. Then, to battle like a champion, you must find tools and resources within yourself. You cannot reach them unless you lose the mask. You have hidden strengths inside your hidden self. You will find them.

> *They fear that if they toss out the masks, they may lose their edge, their competitiveness, and their earning capacity. Lose the masks and they might become soft.*

Remember the Tolstoy quote at the top of this chapter about getting off a man's back? It represented, of course, how we need to get off the back of society. But it also means *we have to get off our own backs.*

Stop driving yourself in an endless pursuit of perfection, competition, and earning more. Resist filling empty spaces of time—the stoplight, the waits at appointments—stop filling them with distractions like your phone. Instead allow for more reflection, go inwards, be with your thoughts, your feelings, your being. That grappling that we have referenced with society is the same skill necessary to be with what is happening inside of us.

Avoid the temptation to succumb to polarities as a way to make sense of the world and what is happening inside of

71

you. Don't drive wedges into complex truths to split them into sides. Don't make false dichotomies like this overheard nugget: "Are the George Floyd protests about racism or police brutality? Why won't they make up their mind?" Forced polarity frees you from having to really consider the larger more nuanced and complex issues, keeping you trapped behind your mask.

We can change these habits of destructive dodging that keeps us men estranged from ourselves and estranged in our relationships. It's just a matter of facing own humanness and exploring our core. It's just a matter of resisting the inhumanity of our masks. Those are just roles we've adopted from society and not our true authentic selves. As adults, we aren't responsible for the programming we downloaded from the world around us. But we are responsible for the upgrades, for installing the new software that shows up on our screen. So much of what is happening in the world around us today is that new software, that new upgrade ready to be downloaded. To begin, all you really have to do is click "yes" and your grappling journey will begin.

And we must do it. Becoming a master of inhumanity by practicing it toward oneself means you end up expressing it in the world. No wonder so much seems wrong. As White men, we are for the most part, the decision makers in this country. We hold the power that could move society forward or keep it stuck in the past, in old ways of being, in sexism and racism.

In the beginning of the chapter, I talked about the original sin of racism and the original sin of sexism. Both can be laid at our feet, not just as inherited notions we can age out of as we evolve as a society but as ongoing sins. They occur when we don't want to share power, when we want exclusion in favor of ourselves. We have constructed a society that relies on sin to distribute the spoils of freedom. Of course, that spoils freedom itself. Freedom and hate are natural adversaries.

One of the more profound moments in my life happened when I was a young man, about twenty-five or twenty-six years old. I was in San Francisco, attending an alternative church with a friend. As we sat listening in the pew, the pastor laid out the Biblical story about original sin, the narrative I was so familiar with. Adam, Eve, punishment, banishment, sin as the basis for our world.

And then she paused, she studied us. Then she asked, "What would the world be like if we built it on the original love?"

Original love. What? "God is Love"

It blew my mind. It blew my heart. Immediately, the implications of her question hit me: If we built a world on the fundamental human capacity to love, we'd be living from the innate goodness that lives inside of us, the goodness that gives us the capacity to love.

I enjoy the writings of David Brooks. He speaks to the reality that we each possess a core essence, an intuition and authenticity, and inner wisdom and deep knowing that is perfect and pure and innately good. That's original love. Part of the problem with us White men is our predictable response to these kinds of discussions of our human nature—that place of feeling and depth—we react as if it's all airy-fairy and beneath our standing as Men. Of course, this marginalization is convenient since we haven't the first clue about how to navigate any of that. We don't want to admit we need a map or that it's time to ask for directions.

But I've seen big, strong men who come into the Hoffman process and have that experience of connecting to their innate goodness in a cellular way; it's an embodied experience. They can move. They can learn. They can grow. When people learn to tap into their core, they can do anything. They can consider anything—grapple with anything—because they can let go. They've been liberated from outmoded thoughts and patterns that have curtailed their lives. They realize, "I don't have to fight you on this. I don't have to fight you on that. I don't have to defend this. I can let go of that." Anything's possible when people don't have to fight for their own worthiness.

As men, we're socialized into what should matter to us, and that programming says we have to continually achieve, fight, win—win everything. We've got to earn it all, our spot in the White male club. But when you can let go of earning "hustle for your worthiness" as Brené Brown says, and instead hold yourself as valuable and worthy no matter who you are or what you do, no matter your external accoutrements, you can be free. That freedom might sound trite at this point, but it is a tangible thing. It involves having a deep sense of choice in how you live your life. Purposeful choices can create profound personal meaning.

In the next chapter, we're going to start learning how to grapple so you can move away from the superficial world of socialization and into your own deep, rich life. I'll teach you about two grappling hooks you need in your toolbelt if you're going to move toward authoring your own life, living out your own values, and having an impact in the world. These grappling hooks will help you get over the walls you've built inside yourself, the socialization that blocks your path toward your own authentic and powerful inner core, the real you.

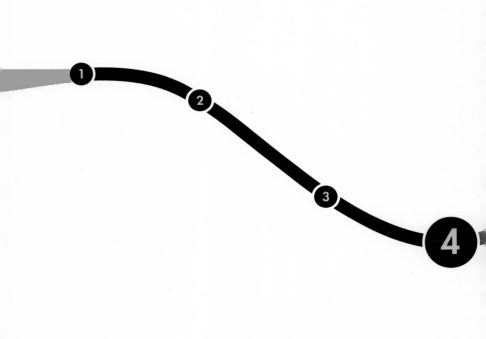

THE GRAPPLING HOOK OF LEARNING

"The one thing I want our company to be incredible at, the one skill I want us to build, is our capacity to learn. It's the cycle of observe, learn, improve. If we can be incredible at that cycle, I'm confident we'll do the right things, no matter what challenges we're facing. If we become too rigid in coming up with an idea..., we're going to become more irrelevant and even dangerous. And we just can't afford that.... I would agree that we haven't been awesome, but I think we're getting better and better every single day, and I think that is on display publicly, especially in this past year around everything that we've learned and how we have evolved our policies and evolved our actions and our enforcement."

—Jack Dorsey, Twitter CEO

Cap

We men love to know. We love to explain. We love to share our knowledge with others. In fact, we're encouraged to be know-it-alls. Knowledge is power, after all. And our socialization is such that we feel compelled to push our knowledge on everyone around us, mansplaining and rarely aware of it. But how did we even get all this knowing?

We know because we learn.

The most successful companies acknowledge this. Jack Dorsey and Twitter are constantly learning because they have no other choice. They are constantly grappling with those who exploit Twitter for misinformation in many different ways, including those asserting an alternate reality. They have to constantly learn how to adjust their settings and algorithms. And as a result, they constantly and consistently get better.

Not so for most of us. Men have been conditioned to move away from learning. Over time our love of knowing weakens that learning muscle that first turned us into knowers. We forget how to take in and process unfamiliar information. We don't know how to make new choices. We don't know how to grow. We veer toward familiarity. We avoid the unknown. The consequence: we end up reliving our past over and over, stuck in a kind of vicious cycle, while the world changes around us. We become irrelevant in our own lives. As philosopher Eric Hoffer put it: "In times of change, learners inherit the earth, while the learned find themselves beautifully equipped to deal with a world that no longer exists."

We must learn how to learn again as we did when we were small. Part of that learning is to unlearn many of the things we were taught, including the power of questions over answers. We must acknowledge that learning is the most important aspect of knowing—and that learning means accepting that we don't always have answers. We don't always know how to fix something. Our opinion is not a substitute for understanding.

Learning helps move us into the unknown and helps us grow. To truly learn, we first must find comfort in the unknown. Too often we associate safety with comfort, when we need to think of the two as separate entities. Discomfort may make us feel unsteady, but it can be very safe. In fact, in the long run, it's very safe to stay in a state of unsteady discomfort, because it means that you want to learn to adapt and learn to be nimble. If you can stay in that state long enough to take in new information or understand a new way of thinking, you learn. You grow. Learning and evolving become the norm rather than the place we are forced to be because of some situation or person that put us there. Being a learner puts us in the driver's seat of our own life.

THE SHITTY FIRST DRAFT

A lot of our resistance to learning is rooted in what author Anne Lamott calls the "shitty first draft." It's the story our mind reflexively tells when confronted by difficult feelings such as anxiety or sudden loss. Often the stories include negative beliefs about ourselves or others. Our mind creates them so that we have a mythology to explain what has happened. That gives us a sense of understanding, no holes to fall through, which in turn lets us feel safe and more in control.

Unfortunately, the first draft our brains throw down are shitty: My teenage daughter isn't answering her phone. For hours. Oh, my God, she's dead in a ditch, maybe being eaten by coyotes. Knocked on my boss's door hoping to talk to him about a raise. He's engrossed in his work, barely looks up at me, and asks, pointedly it seems to me, "Can it wait?" "Sure," I say, unsettled. By that night, I've polished my resume and put out feelers in my network.

But my daughter isn't being eaten. Her phone battery died so she couldn't tell me that a college recruiter was at her school and she had gotten a meeting.

And my boss wasn't getting ready to fire me, sick of my intrusions. No, he was having difficulty with the spreadsheets in front of him because he'd mistakenly put in his wife's contact lenses.

Shitty first drafts can be really shitty.

In order to learn and grow, we have to look out for these SFDs. We have to stop defending them, because they are often riddled with errors and snap judgments. We have to use the more mature, conscious, empowered side of ourselves to challenge the SFDs and figure out how to steer our story in a more positive direction. When we challenge our SFDs, we say, "I'm going to make mistakes. I'm going to fall down. I'm here to eventually get it right, not to *be* right."

If we are constantly trying to *be* right, then we will only step into situations that are familiar. This means we resist making mistakes; we strive to be perfect because making a mistake would be uncomfortable. Perfectionism is the enemy of real learning, because if we never make a mistake, we never learn. We miss the value of errors, and the value of struggle, and the value of not knowing. If we refuse to go back and revise our SFDs, that means we aren't willing to admit or make a mistake. If we quash any thoughts and feelings that don't feel good, it restricts our ability to fall, get back up, learn, and grow. We must allow for the deeper truth of a SFD. Expressing it, even if messy, gives us a chance to sort through it all to find the nuggets of truth.

Those Shitty First Drafts are often full of information gaps, like stick drawings passing for a full color rendering. Ian Leslie, the author of *Curious: The Desire to Know and Why Your Future Depends on It*, says these information gaps cause us pain. They're like an itch we have to scratch. We can do two things with this pain. We can resist it. Or we can welcome it, invite it in, and allow ourselves the discomfort so that we can ask questions and learn and grow and understand. Fewer and fewer people allow themselves to be truly curious and ask provocative questions—or really any questions at all. Which means, of course, they don't know the answers. They are more likely to make snap judgments—or to seek a scapegoat.

yes!

Curiosity is actually an innate quality. It is an emotion that is just as fundamental as anger or love. However, to lean into it, to feed it, means that we must overcome the discomfort of not understanding, not knowing. This discomfort is actually the ground on which we can learn, the foundation on which we can grapple.

its an emotion?

CHANGING YOUR MINDSET

For too long, too many of us have operated under what psychologist Carol Dweck calls a "fixed mindset." We've regarded our brain power as fixed and static, which means we're either smart or we're not; that we have a high IQ and will achieve in life, or we won't. This assumption has a number of harmful effects. It makes us feel as though everything is pre-determined, so we never achieve our full potential. We assume our brain power will never increase, so we don't see a point in making an effort. We avoid challenges. We ignore or chafe at any negative feedback from others, and we feel threatened and jealous by the success of our peers. We grow rigid in our beliefs.

In order to learn and grow, we need to shift our mindset to view intelligence as something that can be developed. Dweck calls this view a "growth mindset." When we think that our brains have potential, we have a desire to learn more, and a tendency to embrace challenges rather than run away from them. We value effort, perseverance, and persistence. We can begin to value criticism and regard it as a gateway to learning, and we can find lessons and inspiration in the success of others. We feel that we have free will, as opposed to determined destiny. We have faith in ourselves to learn and grow.

DRAWING LINES

Once we have this faith to learn, we can begin to extend this learning to all areas of our lives. We can do this by ending the common practice of compartmentalizing parts of our lives. Professional, personal, your community, your world: look at all of these as a whole. Breaking these walls and beginning the process of seeing our lives on a big-picture scale is called "associative learning," and it can be a powerful start to the grappling move of learning.

For instance: perhaps you reacted angrily to something your wife said. If you thought a bit about why you were so angry, you could trace it back to your general feeling of powerlessness in your marriage. You can realize that you feel that your children don't listen to you, either. You can remember how you lashed out at a co-worker, too, and perhaps that's because you felt your voice doesn't matter. You could realize that you act angrily when you feel powerless. If you extended this to the protests for civil justice that you've been reading about, you can connect your reaction to how so many Black people are angry. You can realize the extent to which they, too, feel powerless, and have for centuries because of the legacy of slavery.

Making connections and associations, identifying themes, helps you move about the world as the line connecting all of the dots. Over time, you can do this intentionally. But you can also start by leaning into the discomfort of situations that challenge your identity, whether they're problems in your personal life or upheaval in the news. Resist the urge to cling to your same old ways, to try to put your life back together the way it used to be. Instead, try embracing the change. Rumble with the discomfort that this change creates within yourself and in your life.

Ponder that perhaps this discomfort can be accompanied by comfort, too. The days after the killing of George Floyd were some of the most difficult I've ever experienced as an American. I also found profound beauty and inspiration in watching the protests and how our country came together to demand change. The heartbreak of Floyd's death and inspirational coming together in protest were true, at the same time.

Embrace the "both." Don't fall for the "either/or." As Carl Jung, the founder of analytic psychology, put it, "The paradox is one of our most valued spiritual possessions." It helps us understand that all of us are human, all of us are more than just one thing, identity, or label.

A good example of a paradox is Thomas Jefferson, the third U.S. president. Jefferson badly wanted his legacy to be threefold: he wanted to be remembered for writing the Declaration of Independence, founding the University of Virginia, and authoring Virginia's statute on religious freedom. However, Jefferson's *real* legacy also includes a prominent role in our country's legacy of slavery and racism: he was a lifelong slave owner who fathered children with one of those slaves. Consider this for a moment: how can Jefferson, one of our country's most well-known founding fathers, write these incredible documents, leave behind all of these civic achievements, and also father children with someone he enslaved? How can we accept and acknowledge all these sides of him?

I find myself acknowledging the paradoxes of our country every Independence Day. Each year on July 4, I always display an American flag in my yard, and I enjoy passing out little American flags, too. Sometimes my liberal neighbors see my display of patriotism, raise their eyebrows and say, "Dude, what are you doing?"

Here's how I reply: "Look, I love the United States. I'm incredibly proud of this beautiful, amazing country." I allow myself this patriotism because I fully embrace the paradox of this country. I feel its great accomplishments. I also feel its legacy of oppression and killing. I feel the way the United States government enslaved generations of African Americans, stole sacred lands in the domination of Native Americans, and interned the Japanese during World War II. Like Jefferson's legacy is both admirable and horrific, so is that of the United States. And so, too, is that of our internal world.

The grappling move of cultivating a learner mentality will reveal things that seem mutually exclusive, that can't seem to exist in the same person or the same country. Embracing these paradoxes will help you grapple in more ways than one. Realizing that Jefferson was a human being with many facets helps us remember that we are human, too. When we stop demonizing people, when we stop seeing others only in black or white, as only good or bad, we allow for our own humanity. We allow ourselves to be beautiful beings who are also fraught with conflicting behaviors and feelings, complex people who sometimes say one thing and act another way. Part of grappling is allowing all of this gap, this tension in ourselves, in other people, and in our country.

We allow ourselves to be beautiful beings who are also fraught with conflicting behaviors and feelings, complex people who sometimes say one thing and act another way.

The fundamental nature of grappling is to embrace the paradox and keep working with both sides until you get to some clarity. To do this, you have to think critically, and you have to display a certain amount of judgment. I'm sure you've heard others say "Don't be judgmental," or chiding themselves for being too judgmental. But, in fact, there is value to making a discerning judgment. We don't want to really strive to live in a judgment-free world with no labels. What are we supposed to do, just accept everything people tell us as fact? The goal is to notice our judgments, but don't stop there. Continue to allow new information to enter into our brains and our hearts. We should continue our curiosity, perception, and most of all our learning.

This is a new way of thinking and growing. But when you embrace it, you can begin to enjoy the fruits of the paradox. You can leave behind the superficial comfort that you sought in your previous life, and begin to find a deeper, more profound comfort.

LIVING ON THE EDGE

When I am struggling with new insights, I find it helpful to pinpoint my growth edge. I put my fingers down on the metaphorical spot between What I Know and What I Don't Know. This is the place that's shaded in gray shadows, between the part that's light with my insights, and the part that's dark with what I don't know.

As Ian Leslie said in *Curiosity*, "Curiosity requires an edge of uncertainty to thrive." You may find that the more you learn, the more you want to push your growth edge out. For instance, if you read a particularly thought-provoking book, your curiosity is somewhat sated once you get to the end. However, this book may have provoked more curiosity in you, so you keep reading and learning more and more on the same topic, pushing your growth edge farther out.

Here are some helpful phrases that will automatically extend your growth edge: "I don't know." "That's a good question." "That's an interesting thought." These phrases can broaden your horizons and break you out of the old, destructive cycle of only choosing what you know.

I see this cycle all the time in the couples I work with: when people are faced with a crossroads, they often choose the familiar option. They choose the suffering and pain of the known over any unknown future, even when it's clear this choice won't improve their lives. The known misery is the path chosen over the mystery and adventure of the unknown. Every time we resist the unfamiliar, we're acknowledging our fragility. It might be unconscious, but that choice is an acknowledgment that we can't handle ourselves in a new situation, that we might crash and burn. That we can't fight. That we're scared, and we can't handle that fear.

How did change become such a four-letter word?

We need to stop fearing change. We need to learn to choose discomfort, and encourage others to do so, too. Yes, these changes can feel as though they threaten the very core of your identity. They feel hard and scary. But let's stop thinking of life as something that should be easy. In fact, life is difficult. It can be a struggle. Leaning into this struggle offers you the chance for a stronger sense of confidence and self-respect, a deeper connection to who you really are, a stronger sense of how you can move in the world.

Once we choose to hone these grappling skills, then we can work through anything: issues in our marriage, issues in society, issues at work. The process of each is the same: push through the discomfort to embrace change. Keep going until we get it right and get to the other side of the discomfort that change naturally brings.

This means learning to react to emotional triggers in a way that is not defensive. When you react defensively to your wife telling you she's unhappy, or your boss giving you feedback you don't like, you're investing a lot of energy in keeping things status quo while the people around you are trying to help you grow. Instead of resisting these triggers, we need to look at them as an opportunity for growth and begin to engage with them. That's how we can truly grow.

LEADING WITH YOUR STRENGTH

You won't master all aspects of grappling immediately. If you're feeling overwhelmed, think about your strongest quality. Use that as a keyhole to begin to unlock the process. For instance, if you know yourself to be deeply self-compassionate, then you may have an easier time learning to embrace your mistakes. You'll have an easier time altering that Shitty First Draft. Or, perhaps you know you are open-minded, and you can start by learning to hold two truths at once. If you have deep courage, you can step more deeply into unfamiliarity. If you're comfortable with doing things imperfectly, you can jump right into grappling without making sure you're doing it exactly as you should.

Those of us with humility often have the easiest transition into grappling: we can more easily allow ourselves to admit when we don't know something.

Of course, we all have weaknesses that we carry through that keyhole. We need to make sure those weaknesses do not

THE GRAPPLING HOOK OF LEARNING

define us. We need to grapple with them before they grapple with us. That way we can shape the narrative and tone of our own lives, rather than have the narrative shape us.

YOUR UNCONSCIOUS

Nice summ. of uncon

Grappling is very much rooted in the psychological concept of the unconscious: we aren't aware of everything that we think or feel. Just because you don't understand or know these thoughts doesn't mean they don't exist. Acknowledging that there is a lot happening beneath the surface of us all eases the emergence of these thoughts into the light of our conscious minds. And we can learn to trust them and ourselves.

When people won't grapple, sometimes I think it might be linked to not believing that there is an unconscious. A big part of grappling involves welcoming this unconscious and trying to make meaning of it. Humans are innately meaning makers, trying to make meaning of our lives, but sometimes we aren't aware that we are doing so. We just continue to tell ourselves the same stories, finding meaning in the same Shitty First Drafts, without really exploring what's behind, around, and under them and writing new narratives.

Right

To start the learning process, the first step is to explore what's in your head. Just throw it all out there. What is the story you tell yourself about your life? What are the familiar themes, and scenes, and lines? For some of my clients, it may be something as "life sucks," or "life is hard." When they tell me that, I help them explore that story. We extend it to what's happening in their marriage, in their parenting, at their jobs. We try to understand and make meaning in their lives. It's understanding their own story, and why they tell themselves the same narrative.

Once we understand our own narratives, then we can grapple with them, and determine the kind of authentic meaning we want to make from it. We can reflect on the path we've been on. We can ask ourselves whether we chose this path, or whether we were born into it. We can embrace the paradoxes of our own lives that we may not have had total control over, that we are a product of the status and system we were raised in, and also that this status and system brought us a lot of good things. We can acknowledge the events and circumstances that influenced our lives and shaped our minds into what they are today.

An important but uncomfortable step in grappling happens when we unlearn some of the lessons of our past, when we realize we don't have to think like our parents thought. All of the steps we've discussed in this chapter—learning, exploring, having a growth mindset, and making authentic meaning—automatically challenge our white-male socialization. They mean we can stop reacting reflexively and start bringing intention to the life we want to live.

FEELING THE DISCOMFORT

People who don't grapple often don't see the world and themselves in a nuanced way. They may provide simplistic answers, or they may have fashioned a kind of alternative reality with lots of theories. What they never come right out and say is that their reactions are often rooted in fear.

In order to learn, you have to get past that fear, past these strong emotions, so that you are not afraid to step beyond anything in your way. We have to channel our growth mindset beyond learning itself but include our feelings about learning. As Flannery O'Connor once said, "The truth does not change according to our ability to stomach it emotionally."

Feelings can interfere with learning. They distract us. They pull us back from opening up our minds and our hearts. In the next chapter, we'll explore feelings as the second grappling hook that can take you over the internal walls built by socialization.

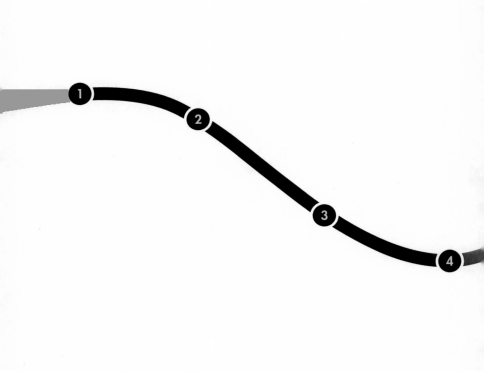

THE GRAPPLING
HOOK OF FEELING

"(Y)our vision will become clear only when you can look into your own heart. Without, everything seems discordant; only within does it coalesce into unity. Who looks outside dreams; who looks inside awakes."
—Carl Jung, *C. G. Jung Letters, Vol.1: 1906-1950*

I n order to successfully grapple with the challenges of our lives, we men must allow ourselves to feel and begin to understand and accept what we are feeling. I know this because I lived it.

From the time I was in elementary school, I always felt different. I had a deep connection to my emotional world. I always felt things more intensely than most other guys, who were hyper-competitive. I was competitive, too, but not like them. They enjoyed beating the bejesus out of each other, and their behavior reminded me of the aggressive *Tom and Jerry* cartoons that I found hard to watch.

I reserved all of my masculine boy energy for sports. The basketball court seemed like a place to express this energy safely and effectively. But I still struggled with the culture of confrontation, teasing, and sarcasm that went along with the sport. When I was in middle school, I remember a rival athlete making fun of my skills. "We're going to take you," he taunted me relentlessly. I didn't know how to react. When I shared this with my father, Dad told me to respond, "I'll see you on the court."

Although I struggled with competitive verbal banter, I loved and excelled in the competitive physical play of basketball, so I followed Dad's advice. It worked. But matching my rival's competitive language didn't feel satisfying to me. It just felt uncomfortable.

I always felt like more of a mama's boy. I led a sheltered life. I went to a small school and spent a lot of time with my family. I was close to my younger brother, who was a sweet and gentle little guy. My mother exposed me to a lot of art and music. I also connected deeply to characters in film and TV. And I felt a connection to some of my parents' heroes from the 1960s protest movements, such as Martin Luther King Jr. and Robert F. Kennedy. My parents' ideals were lived in our home, part of our family's identity. For instance, they adopted a Vietnamese orphan whose parents had been killed in the Vietnam War.

We were a happy family with love in our household, but no family is without its bumps. I had a conflicted relationship with my parents, the emotional son who society insisted should limit self-expression to acceptable "manly" displays. Years later, as I tried to work out why my parents had raised me as they had, I sat down with them to share some problematic memories. They saw my pain, and their response to it was humbling. They pointed out how different I was from my siblings and then said, "We didn't know what we were doing. We didn't have a manual. We were just trying to figure it out as we went along."

I was trying to figure it out, too. Over time, I learned to play a role: the heart-centered but overwhelmed and spastic kid who excelled as an athlete but fell short in the classroom. I fell into that role so much so that I internalized it. It became a kind of identity for me. I didn't go down the repressed feelings route a lot of guys follow. I couldn't. I had a strong connection to my feelings, and willingly shared them.

But I was feeling too much. I needed help engaging and containing my feelings to keep up with school. I wanted to learn but couldn't seem to figure out how to do so. I had such a hard time focusing and concentrating. I became emotionally volatile and reactionary and impulsive. Over time, my role in life began to confuse me. I knew something more was out there.

By the time I was ready to choose a high school, my bad grades indicated I needed extra help. For that reason, my parents sent me to a boarding school. Even though I agreed with the decision, I felt cast out and a bit lost as I showed up on campus as a fifteen-year-old.

What none of us recognized at the time was that I didn't actually need academic help. I needed emotional help. I needed to clear out emotional blocks, settle my heart down, make room in my brain to take in and digest data and information. In his book *Permission to Feel,* Dr. Marc Brackett provides conclusive data that our emotional system is inextricably linked to our cognitive system and our attention. He has founded the Yale Center for Emotional Intelligence, trying to help teachers understand the role of emotions in successful learning in the classroom. That wasn't going on at my new school.

An all-boys boarding school was a spectacularly bad fit for me. All the school did was give me a PhD in Guy Code. I had no role models for emotions, aside from one English teacher who teared up when he read from the text we were studying. At the time, the school had few outlets for creative expression such as a music or arts program. I had played the violin in middle school, but there was nowhere to do that here. I got excited in my junior year when the school started a chorus, but it was run by the assistant football coach and never really went anywhere after a few practices.

The school had few female teachers, and even fewer adults who displayed any real feelings. My algebra teacher was so "masculine" that he once threatened to throw a student out the window. We boys weren't even given the space to feel, including normal feelings of loneliness being away from home for boys so young. I remember the headmaster saying, "You know how you deal with homesickness, boys? You stay busy." So, we did: life was a constant cycle of class, sports, study hall, sleep.

I remember wondering, *Isn't there more to my education than what is happening here?* Nobody talked about what was really going on inside of them, and that felt like a huge elephant in the room for me.

I was a junior in college by the time I decided I'd had enough of my inner turmoil. I could not match my external world with my internal world. My life had turned into a charade. I sought help, telling the therapist I sought after I dropped out of school: "I want what comes out of my mouth to reflect what matches my internal experience. Because right now, I feel like everything I say feels inauthentic."

My life then got worse before it got better. Because my feelings kept interfering with my ability to absorb new information, I had to drop out of school. I needed time to make sense of the world and myself. That's the thing about feelings: they give you a lot of information, but you have to be able to manage them. You have to identify them, process them, understand them, and accept them—a kind of management of feelings. And you have to nurture them and act from them.

Well, I couldn't do any of that. I couldn't tell what I was feeling or how it was any different from what other people were feeling. I was reacting to emotions I didn't know I was even having. Feelings that worked for me when I was young—those I experienced when deeply connected to others and to nature, for instance—had become overwhelming. This internal turmoil had not only interfered with focus to the point I'd become a college drop-out, I couldn't even set boundaries with people in my life. I was so confused by my internal turmoil I couldn't properly navigate friendships and dating. I didn't know who I was in those months and couldn't ask for what I needed. Everything was sucked into the twisting, spiraling feelings inside me.

At first, therapy made me even more anxious and confused. My demons and insecurities got louder and louder. Thankfully, I had a loving and supportive therapist to help me work out all of the questions in my head. Importantly, he helped me see that for a long time I had sat in judgment of myself, asking myself disapproving questions: Why aren't I learning? What's wrong with me? Why couldn't I stick to college? Why did I drop out? Why am I so different? It was a self-punishing voice in my head that had the intention of trying to hold myself accountable. The impact of those overly critical thoughts, however, left me feeling not good enough, that something was wrong with me, and that I was the only one.

What I discovered was that I had internalized a lot of the messages around feelings that the world around me was giving. Later, I realized that those messages are the dominant White straight male world energy that I'd always felt distant from. My inner voice would say, "Suck it up, Andy, deal with it." But when you approach your feelings so militantly, they don't go away. They linger and fester, sometimes even growing stronger, a psychological phenomenon known as the rebound effect. I was stuck in my feelings and they were owning me. I needed to find a way to metabolize them—to digest them to get to the other side. Too often feelings become things we try to avoid or get out of. But the only way out is through. Feelings that aren't metabolized end up being metastasized.

My break from college turned out to be a relief. I no longer had to compete or engage in traditional college behavior that felt even more inauthentic. I had to find a job and pay rent. I found work as a coach and PE assistant teacher at a grade school. Later, I biked around the country with my younger brother, cycling mile after mile, meeting people and moving my body. I slowly began to thaw out from all that had been happening. I began to feel myself within myself. I had done enough processing in my brain about what was happening the bike trip of nearly 10,000 miles became a chance to bring my body online to this new way of being. And with each pedal, I slowly became increasingly free from my past and more connected to the adult I was becoming.

By the time I returned to school, I had sorted through my emotions so they weren't so intrusive in my daily life. I felt less inner conflict and had more internal clarity that then led to more peace and kindness and ease in my life. I realized that I'd been raised a certain way but hadn't stepped into my own sense of the how I wanted to be. Psychologists call it the stage of individuation and it can take many forms. Mine felt delayed and a bit dramatic by dropping out, but looking back, it has proved to be one of the best things, along with the bike trip, that I've ever done in my life.

I was becoming my own person. I was becoming my own person by coming into a new relationship with my emotional world.

THE POWER OF FEELINGS

I am far from the only man who has been brought to personal crisis because I subjugated my own feelings. As therapist and author Lori Gottlieb puts it in her book *Maybe You Should Talk to Someone*:

Men tend to be at a disadvantage here because they aren't typically raised to have a working knowledge of their internal words. It's less socially acceptable for men to talk about their feelings. While women feel cultural pressure to keep up their physical appearance, men feel that pressure to keep up their emotional appearance. Women tend to confide in friends or family members, but when men tell me how they feel in therapy, I'm almost always the first person they've said it to. Like my female patients, men struggle with marriage, self-esteem, identity, success, their parents, their childhoods, being loved and understood—and yet these topics can be tricky to bring up in any meaningful way with their male friends. It's no wonder that the rates of substance abuse and suicide in middle-aged men continue to increase. Many men feel don't feel they have any other place to turn.

Our Guy Code has taught us to brush feelings aside in order to compete, earn, dominate, and win. Many of us have experienced financial payoffs by avoiding our feelings. But we inevitably find that temporary payoff comes with a steep price when we hit painful periods in life: losing our jobs, the death of people close to us, ruptured friendships, and the eruption of protests and movements we don't understand. Those of us who have spent our lives avoiding strong feelings are left with no idea how to deal with these crises, and the result is that we often react in defensive avoidant ways or even impulsive ways.

Emotions aren't meant to sit dammed up in some fetid subterranean pond within us. They're supposed to flow through us and stay fresh. If we let our feels flow, we'll have experience in their sensations. Then we have the freedom to engage with the big events of life. We can relax into living, instead of avoiding or constantly reacting in impulsive ways.

Let me give you another analogy from, of all things, feeding my cats. When the cats' feeding bowl was left on the floor, the dogs ate it, so we began placing the cat food bowl up on the mantle. The cats ate only a bit at a time, and it was easy to forget about bowls of food sitting out of the way on the mantle. We eventually noticed a smell, and when we checked the food, it was covered in maggots.

After some horrified exclamations of, "You gotta see this!" our family discussed how to take care of the cat food in the future, before maggots appeared. We also talked about how those maggots got on the cat food in the first place. I remembered a concept I learned in biology class and in perhaps a mansplaining moment with my kids, shared that centuries ago, people believed in "spontaneous generation:" meat left out seemed to spawn maggots so it appeared as if living organisms came from non-living matter. That the meat actually grew the maggots. In reality, what actually happened was more complicated: flies attracted to the meat laid eggs in it, and the larvae— maggots—emerged from those eggs.

These maggots are a great analogy for feelings. We are so alienated from them that we think feelings just sponta-neously appear, and we shift the blame for them outward to our wives, children, bosses, the traffic, unexpected news. Anything or anyone that was in the area when the feeling appeared. But of course, like spontaneous generation, that's not the real story. We are the source of our feelings despite what strangers our hearts have become. We can own them instead of externalizing them or falsely attributing them to other people or events.

Since we've been so conditioned to hide emotion, when we do get emotional, our reflex can also be to stop, to apolo-gize, to regain self-control. My grandfather, who was born in 1904, lived to see so much and loved to tell us grandchildren all about his life. But invariably, he would get emotional, choke up, and stop telling the story of having to find coal on the train tracks at age nine to heat his house, unsure what would be happening when he got home where he might have to shoulder the caretaker role. It was as if my grandfather had come to a precipice only to back off. Each time, I remember feeling, "Wait, you were just getting to the important part!"

That's what I'm telling you, too. When you start to get emotional, don't stop and don't apologize. Jump into that place. Because in jumping, we can move through it and get to the other side. Yes, this can feel like stepping off a cliff into the abyss. Acknowledge that you are surrendering the comfort of the known, going to places where you can't control the outcome. But the rewards can be so rich. We have to trust that we *can get* to the other side, that we won't get lost in our feelings.

Kevin, a father of two young children and a college professor, found this out at the end of his life. He was diagnosed with a brain tumor that killed him less than ten months later at age fifty-one. Just twelve days before Kevin's death, I sat down for a podcast interview with him and his wife to talk about the end of his life, his legacy, and what he wanted his children to know about him.

Kevin was not a natural grappler with feelings. He grappled in the field of education and equity and learning modalities but less so around his internal emotional world.

I'm grateful he got out of bed and set up with microphones and sat down with his wife—also a college professor—to have this awkward, courageous conversation. Knowing this was his last chance, Kevin found a way to say things he had never said to his wife before, including the immense gratitude he felt for her. And he admitted regret that he did not have more empathy when she struggled with migraines during their marriage. Now with his brain tumor, he had found this understanding. Today, Kevin's wife looks back at that conversation with gratitude for the moment in time it created prior to his death as well as for the recorded memory it leaves for his kids.

You don't have to wait for a grave situation to do this—to grapple. And you don't have to start grappling all at once. You can tiptoe forward inch by inch. But if you never go near that edge of that seeming abyss you've been avoiding, as time passes it will only seem bigger and darker and more threatening.

JUMPING INTO THE ABYSS

I know this leap is not easy. And many of us have to be pushed off our seemingly safe perch in order to begin grappling with the reality of our emotions. Our socialization has taught us to avoid the inward glance. And anyway, looking inward usually doesn't give us the quick practical solution or answer that we crave. In fact, things can feel more complicated as they did for me when I entered therapy during what were supposed to be my carefree college years. It is choosing a longer, more circuitous route. But as a Persian poet and mystic advised, "Don't turn away, keep your gaze on the bandaged place, that is where the light enters you."

Though grappling can initially cause confusion, it also gives us something powerful if we make the commitment—the opportunity to access the depth and fullness of our soul. When we engage in this kind of reckoning, we discover a world full of much more color and light than we had remembered from our earliest years, the years before socialization started to turn our worlds to monochrome. We were all born in the light, but over time, we become blind to it. Grappling lets us see it again.

When we engage in this kind of reckoning, we discover a world full of much more color and light than we had remembered from our earliest years, the years before socialization started to turn our worlds to monochrome.

You might start by recognizing that all feelings have value, especially the hard ones, even when they are inconvenient or seem inappropriate. The old paradigm on feelings is that there are positive and negative feelings. But we now know that a feeling isn't the problem, it's how we relate to it that becomes the problem. For example, on a recent trip to visit my in-laws, I was overwhelmed with a feeling of missing my parents. It came as a total surprise, because I don't have pangs over missing my parents. On that trip, I had wanted to be present with my wife and my in-laws, to focus on being a son-in-law. But then came the longing for my own parents.

To come back to being present in the present, I had to accept my feelings of longing and sadness about my own family. I had to acknowledge that the feelings were meaningful and relevant; they weren't just spontaneously generated out of the blue. I had to reckon with these emotions, these windows into my unconscious, and realize that behind my feelings lay a strong desire to reconnect with my mom and dad. I was feeling a deep sense of fragility about their lives during a time of pandemic that impacts older people. Discovering what my heart understood informed my decision to find a safe way to visit them.

Too often, we investigate feelings as if there needs to be a "why?" to them. That why might eventually be clear to us, but trying too hard too quickly can dilute or misdirect us from the value the feelings themselves have for us, bringing us to an overly analytical place. Instead of allowing ourselves to feel and understand, we try to take intellectual control. Instead of getting stuck in the intellect, just allow your feeling to be for ninety seconds. Neuroanatomist Jill Bolte Taylor, author of the memoir *My Stroke of Insight: A Brain Scientist's Personal Journey*, tells us that when a person expresses an emotion, a ninety-second chemical process occurs in the body. If you look at it and feel it for ninety seconds, a feeling will move away on its own. If it doesn't, you're in an emotional loop and will need to examine the thoughts you're using to keep the feeling alive.

Lawyer Bryan Stevenson once said, "It's that mind-heart connection that I believe compels us to not just be attentive to all the bright and dazzling things but also the dark and difficult things." If I had ignored the sadness I'd been feeling, shoved it away and tried to distract myself, I would have missed the chance to hear the wisdom of my own heart. What it came down to was enjoining me to connect with my parents in tenuous times, just in case. To avoid regret. The "dark and difficult" in that way was transformed to light and connection.

BIGOTRY TURNED INWARD

Disavowing our feelings not only cuts us off from the wisdom they offer us but makes us unable to effectively manage and control them, as was the case for me in college. We end up developing a hard outer shell. The net effect of that shell, that rigidity, is internal fragility. We can't cope with difficult, emotion-provoking situations. We feel frustrated by them, defensive, and often reactive. Which is how White fragility so often looks like bigotry. When we push away issues that make us White men uncomfortable—sometimes with a lot of force—how can it not be mistaken for bigotry or misogyny, especially to others of us who *can* sit with difficult issues in order to understand? Meanwhile, women and people of color feel the fatigue of harassment and injustice, hearing men complain about how tired they are of "dealing" with social issues exemplifies men's sense of entitlement. It is proof that we have privilege, and is tone deaf, callous, and feels like prejudice, since it means we assume everyone else is there to make us more comfortable.

Bigotry is such a dark thing. It scuttles in the shadows, unwelcomed by most of us. Yet, here we are, with our messy biases and ignorance and fear, no matter how well-meaning we are. Though we generally agree that bigotry should be eradicated, many of us cannot do that within ourselves. Bigotry, bias, selective perception, confirmation bias—it's all been ingrained.

We *can* make a start through grappling with our emotions, but here's the thing: we are actually bigoted against our emotions, too. We've been socialized to believe that intellect is inherently superior. In reality, though, feelings are more powerful than the intellect. You can't always rely on intellect to guide you to your truth: start with an incorrect premise and you end up with an incorrect conclusion. And thoughts can be manipulated, as we all know from having been socialized.

Feelings are deeper, more complicated, and they have a mind of their own. You can rely on your feelings if you take the time to understand them. They tell you the truth about yourself. It's important to know that feelings are messages from you to you and about you. Without that understanding, you might attribute some external reason for your discomfort because you're only seeing surface feelings, and not what those feelings are pointing to within. You're likely to fall into and run with a false narrative.

Let's take, for example, walking into a party and feeling uncomfortable. You might not be able to name that discomfort right away. Instead, it might be easier to notice and find fault with the hosts or the other party guests for what you think might be a valid reason. Freud called this defense mechanism "projection." But what if you instead welcomed that feeling of discomfort, engaged with it, and watched where it took you? What if you said to yourself, "I'm really uncomfortable. I feel kind of insecure. Why is that? Is it because that guy's wearing a suit and I feel underdressed? Or is it because I got into a disagreement with my wife before we arrived? Or because I've been thinking a lot about the political situation and it makes me worried? Is it because I'm just feeling really sensitive, that I'm in this kind of sensitive, soulful place right now?" Mindful self-aware-ness of feelings can reroute the direction of your thoughts, and thus change your reactions.

At first, this process is not particularly efficient. It might take a while, and it might not always be practical in real time. Years ago, I was rushing down the freeway taking my family on a hiking outing. My six-year-old was in an "I hate hiking" phase and proclaimed she couldn't go hiking because her knee was hurt.

Being wise to her ways, I assured her that she could. She countered by insisting her knee was really hurt. I continued that the family was going to hike that day. Before I knew it, I'm in a debate with my six-year-old daughter about the merits of hiking, at the same time negotiating traffic as I drive up into the mountains at 70 miles per hour. My daugh-ter is getting more animated and I'm getting more animated. Finally, I just don't know what to do next. I'm stymied, extremely uncomfortable, and I just want it to stop. Before I could juggle my feelings of frustration and helplessness with good driving and the proper parenting of a six-year-old loudly complaining in the back seat, my daughter ups the ante, declaring that her knee is actually broken, so—.

I just laid on the horn.

She tries to speak, tries to say that's not fair. More horn.

I outshout her with the horn three times before I silence her, probably humiliate her, too. I feel slightly better because

I released the tension—the horn was like a pressure release valve. But then I look over at my wife, and I'm filled with shame. Genny is staring at me, shaking her head. Her face tells me *you've got a problem, Andy.*

I'd failed to navigate the moment: there was too much going on to process both my feelings and my daughter's feelings. I should have left the whole situation to my wife, who wasn't driving. I might have also taken a step back instead of engaging and trying to "solve" the situation. There I probably would have been struck by the humor of a six-year-old's creative excuses for why she couldn't hike. As it was, I had to grapple with the mess *not* grappling had created.

From my work and research around men, I knew that I had fallen into a male socialization trap: I needed to fix it (that is, end it and make myself comfortable again), I needed my daughter to make me comfortable by subjugating her own discomfort, and I'd entered into an inappropriate power struggle with her that resulted in an act of aggressive dominance. I could not manage my feelings of irritation and anxiety and being overwhelmed. I had a million choices, but the cost of not doing the work to reconcile feelings creates the impression that you have no choice.

In those moments I had zero agility. I wasn't nimble enough to sidestep what was happening to find a constructive path forward. And I hadn't been able to pick up the cue from my frustration that something deeper was at work:

my hope that we would have a successful outing, create good family memories, laugh together, feel bonded to one another, be a happy family.

Given all this messy, circuitous, and confusing introspection, it's understandable that many of us think, "Why the hell would I go there?"

I get it. But consider this: the world, no matter how we pretend and insulate ourselves, is never going to be neat and straightforward. My daughter wasn't going to turn into an adult overnight, sparing me of the need to gain urgently needed coping skills. Protests against long-standing injustice and grievances are going to keep surging up until we face up to needed change. The world will continue to turn and morph into new social dimensions to reckon with and new standards of what will and won't be tolerated. The sooner we learn to come to terms with our emotions, the sooner we can find more ease and agility with whatever faces us.

It becomes much more efficient as we practice it, as we build up what I call the "moment muscle"—being self-aware in the moment and knowing from that place what to do next. If we can strengthen this muscle of acknowledging or assessing feelings in the moment, we'll all be better off. There's so much to this rich tapestry of our heart. If we don't know what we feel, how can we know what we need?

Grappling is really just putting a positive spin on struggle. Thinking, "Wow, I'm struggling today," sounds passive, like something's happening *to* us and we're just trying to outlast it. But saying, "I'm grappling with this thing" makes us active participants—you're doing something, searching it, assessing it, wrestling with it, figuring it out. Instead of having a bias against your feelings, you're in there with them in the trenches. Your feelings become normal to you, allies describing the situation, not just giving you intel but aiding you in navigating the times you're living in. You're grappling, and grappling is living consciously, agilely, and purposefully. And you know you can get to the other side of your feelings to metabolize them feeling lighter and freer and powerful to navigate the next challenge with greater ease.

BEYOND GOOD AND BAD

Unfortunately, complexity is missing for most men. Most men know only two feelings—good or bad and maybe angry—and their emotional world feels barren from this oversimplification. Instead of color, the world inside and out is black or white.

Competing feelings can exist at the same time, though. You can only truly understand this once you begin to grapple: that two opposite feelings can not only exist, they can exist right next to each other, connected and both true. The graduating senior who is partying and drinking and celebrating can also feel sadness, loss, and remorse that his college experience is coming to an end. The proud new father can also mourn the loss of his care-free, child-free days.

Without the reckoning of naming our feelings, you can't really understand yourself. How can you understand someone you don't get to know? Most men have no idea that their feelings can be so much richer, more varied, and more informative than good or bad. They dread the "bad" emotions that burst through the dam—fear, anger, jeal-ousy, competitiveness—because they can't reckon with them. So-called good feelings are more welcome, but once noticed, they ought not to get too expressive. It leaves men having strange and incomplete dialogues: "'Do you love her?' 'I don't know.'" "'Are you happy?' 'What's happi-ness, anyway?'"

Meanwhile, the emotions beneath good or bad go uncharted, feelings of gentleness, tenderness, protective-ness, poignancy, profundity; the bittersweet, more nuanced feelings that add true dimension and meaning to our days. The feelings that make us appreciate all that life is.

What a terrible disservice we do ourselves. And while we cheat ourselves this way, we hurt our long-term health. What if I hadn't realized that my feelings of sadness while at my in-laws were linked to missing my own parents? What if I had just stopped at a vague label of feeling down or depressed? The feelings wouldn't have just gone away and there they'd be, pulling at me, engaging me, owning me, detracting from my moments.

I'm sure you can recognize that emotional situation because we White men find ourselves there over and over, owned by feelings that won't go away, feelings that refuse to be squashed. They keep returning and buzzing in our heads and annoying us. That "returning" might take minutes or days. Sometimes, we can push feelings down so far that they only eventually return years, even decades later. We get frustrated and, since we don't know how to grapple, we can't tolerate it. It's so commonplace that there's a term for it: low frustration-tolerance. People who have LFT develop a kind of long-term stress in which they're not able to process emotions. It can even turn into debilitating depression and anxiety. White men, socialized and deadened by our privilege, tend to express LFT.

It's ironic that avoiding feelings makes them more powerful than turning towards them and then making choices. Feelings will influence you either way. Might as well own up to them and own them rather than them owning you. Grappling tells the world that you won't let fear overtake you. You're going to face those feelings. You're going to treat them as friend not foe.

Doing so might send you back to a much more tender, vulnerable, younger-seeming state. "I feel like a little kid," some of my clients have said. They think it feels immature, so they judge themselves and move away from feeling.

Let's explore this dynamic. If we haven't grappled with our feelings as we grew up, if we're taught to instead put feelings in a drawer, denying them oxygen and the opportunity to grow, feelings stay in their younger form. Imagine what would have happened if we put our intellect away when we were younger. It, too, would never be exposed to new ideas and new thoughts. The reality is that we can give our emotions the opportunity to grow up as much as our intellect has grown. We can develop coping mechanisms around an emotional state that we're just starting to understand.

It won't always feel confusing or frightening or overwhelming. The more we do this work with our feelings, the less fragile we are. We begin tolerating frustration better and making better choices for ourselves. We move from fragile to agile.

AGILITY

Agility means you can reckon with your feelings and not blame them on the environment. It gives you the courage to allow feelings, to understand, learn, and move them, so that you can eventually move on. You can be present to both your feelings *and* what's happening in the moment.

You can do all of this without blaming or trying to control the situation. You can accept whatever is happening and ask for what you want and need. Psychologist Tara Brach has a helpful acronym for us—RAIN: Recognize, Allow, Investigate, Nurture. Doing those, especially the more you practice, creates a kind of emotional agility.

Agility puts you in control of your life.

Whatever happens—whatever crisis or change might arise—you *will* have the agility to get through it. No matter the terrain—rugged or rocky, hot or dry, snowy or stormy— you can handle it. You can say, "Whoa, this is grief. Isn't that interesting?" or, "Wow, this is a little bit of irritation."

You'll have a deeper connection to yourself. As a result, you have more power and more confidence. Men love confidence and the charisma that comes with it, but too often they try to acquire the accoutrements of confidence without the more challenging work of getting to the other side of the hard emotions that give us true confidence. Confidence is an inside job, and you can only get it by mastering your internal world. That mastery comes from rolling up our sleeves to attend to all that is unsettled in our heart.

Becoming agile also leads to emotional regulation. This is not the same as being self-composed. Learning to emotionally regulate means you feel and express the emotion. You have to be with the emotion and regulate yourself at the same time, having the capacity to know what you need as a result of the feeling. Self-composure is too often about training yourself to compartmentalize the emotion or at least keep a poker face as you try, and this can often backfire. If you don't feel the emotion, it will not dissipate. It will metastasize.

Developing this agility results in learning to be comfortable in discomfort and awkwardness. You have to learn to dance with your emotions instead of just concentrating on looking expressionless all the time. You need your internal and your external world to be partners so that you can dance more smoothly in your head and in your life. You need your feelings to work with you and inform you, rather than trying to assassinate them when they are undesirable.

Part of learning to do this is developing the capacity to delay gratification. Psychiatrist M. Scott Peck's book *The Road Less Traveled* begins thus: "Life is difficult." Peck goes on to say that if you embrace this truth, it becomes no longer relevant. It just becomes life. But if you try to resist it and insist that life should somehow be easier, or you should be entitled to certain things, then you have made life profoundly difficult—bad news for we conditioned men of privilege who believe exactly that: that life is supposed to take it easy on us. No. Life is difficult. It's not going to be all instant gratification.

Same goes for grappling. This shit ain't easy, man. Finding meaning and purpose and joy in life requires so much of us, and it's no overnight feat. If men can learn to delay gratification, they will be richly rewarded. It's like the famous Stanford test in which children are given marshmallows and are told that if they wait, they can have two marshmallows instead of one. Those children who could delay gratification would years later prove to be more well-adjusted and viewed as "competent." They also had higher SAT scores. Emotional intelligence enables grappling, gifting you patience, higher frustration tolerance, grit—gifts that facilitate success.

Another bonus of developing agility is that once we possess it, we can share it with others. As a therapist, I know the importance of catching the nuances of others' emotions and also managing my own. Agility enables us to do that—to understand what emotions other people are expressing or feeling, to be intuitive enough to understand what someone else is experiencing. Your interactions can go to a whole new level of constructiveness and cooperation if you first learn to allow for and understand others this way. Daniel Goleman outlined this in his landmark book *Emotional Intelligence*, reporting that EQ stood above IQ as a predictor of success.

Imagine if I had done that with my six-year-old years ago instead of screaming by way of my horn. This control and aggression can look like strength on the outside. It can also be experienced as rigidity. Can you consider that your failure to come to terms with your internal world has created regimented ways that you show up externally? And to go a step further, that how you view the world can be rigid in response to that lack of internal reckoning?

In referencing the power that White people have had over Black peoples' lives for over 400 years, Isabel Wilkerson, author of *Caste*, among other books, reflects on the defensiveness of White people around racism that "perhaps... is one of the central points. Because it is so fragile it is defended with such force and such rigidity. Maybe underneath it all people do know in their heart or mind how fragile this is, this is not real, this is built on such a fragile foundation and belief system that one single thing could turn it in a different direction, that there is no basis for it and so one would defend it all the more."

SHAME, AND WHAT FOLLOWS

If I don't have faculty around my emotion, then I think other people are the cause of it. So, I externalize. I end up feeling victimized by others, those who evoked those emotions.

Often, the underlying reason for all of this is a deep sense of shame. White men are often socialized in such a way that shame surrounds our deepest core. We can never live up to the "ideal" man whose feelings are beside the point, interferences in a life of earning and competition, of doing, owning, and then, if there's time left, being. We know we can never be perfect. We can have at the heart of us an existential feeling of unworthiness.

Shame is the intensely painful experience or feeling of being flawed and therefore unworthy of love and belonging. Some describe it as "unwanted identity." Shame can resonate so strongly in our body as a sensation that it feels like an indictment of our being. If guilt is "I made a mistake," shame is "I *am* a mistake." However it's described in research, we hardly ever talk about it. Try sharing with someone a bit about your shame and see what happens. Note the look on the other person's face.

But shame is a part of our humanity, and the taboo against naming and sharing your shame is harmful. Shame thrives in darkness but evaporates in the light. And shame hates being named and shrinks from it. That makes it vital that we to go toward our feelings of shame with courage and compassion. We must name shame and shrink it so we don't end up taking feelings of shame out on ourselves or others. White men's feelings of shame over the misogyny and racism of the past and present mean they avoid these topics. Trying to avoid shame serves as a deterrent to shouldering responsibility and becoming a change agent, which doesn't benefit anyone.

Shame is different than guilt. Guilt is the feeling that we did something wrong, something that goes against who we are. Guilt can actually be a healthy behavior modifica-tion: when we feel guilt, we can change things for the better. Shame, by contrast, is the feeling not that we've done some-thing wrong, but that we *are* wrong. And it doesn't correlate to being able or worthy of doing anything to change it.

Good news: dealing with shame is a key step in grap-pling. We have to allow the feeling of shame when it comes. Shame doesn't like its name spoken, so we need to say it out loud: "Oh, this is shame," so that it can dissipate. Putting light on shame takes away its power. It can require a lot of discomfort, because the physical sensations of shame mir-ror trauma. Whether you've been in a car crash or you've only been pulled over by the police, your body doesn't often know the difference and can treat both the same—hands sweat, heart beats, voice shakes.

Although no feelings are bad, shame is one that can really take us down. And some people are more prone to shame than others. What we want to do is separate the sin from the sinner. We need to say, "I'm a good person who made a bad choice by tearing down the shed." Or, "I'm a good person who made a bad choice by not considering the feelings of my college girlfriend." We can acknowledge, "I was temporarily an asshole. That's not who I am. That's not who I want to be toward others."

We want to recognize that shame is there, but we are not our shame. Pretending shame isn't there doesn't make it go away, but just allows it to fester. Shame thrives with a sense of unworthiness, with our struggle to be worthy. We need to develop resiliency around it.

Open to the shame as it appears in your life. Wrestle with it, knowing it's not you. That allows it to dissipate. Don't believe that you deserve it. Hold yourself accountable, allow others to hold you accountable, but do not believe you are unworthy because you made a mistake. That dehumanization will only perpetuate shame.

The failure to grapple with our own shame has grave ramifications for the social justice movement. For White men, the road forward is narrowing more and more. We're being held accountable for our history and the role of White men in slavery and racism and misogyny. We're being held accountable by women and by Black and brown people.

Here's what's important to know about this. *Feeling* shame as we are held accountable for racism and sexism is not the same thing as *being* shamed. If we are experiencing shame, that's our responsibility. We cannot externalize and blame this shame on those who are holding us accountable.

In one famous example, Florida GOP Congressman Ted Yoho insulted New York Democratic Congresswoman Alexandra Ocasio-Cortez after a tense exchange, calling her a "fucking bitch." When Ocasio-Cortez publicly rebuked him on the House floor, many people said that she shamed Yoho. But she didn't shame Yoho: she held him accountable.

It's the combination of being an ethnic minority as a Puerto Rican, a woman, and a person of color that enabled her to eloquently express how Yoho's words were emblematic of the systematic attempt to shame those who don't belong to the White Male Club. And to excuse it. Indeed, Ocasio-Cortez only decided to publicly rebuke Yoho when he used his wife and daughters to shield himself from his clear-cut display of misogyny.

Why was it clear cut? He confronted her rudely. She stood up for herself as an equal, pointed out his rudeness, and walked away on her original business. When she did not try to appease him, he used violent language to label her as defective. He could not tolerate her because he could not tolerate his frustration. This is the future for those of us who refuse to navigate for the sake of clarity our own internal assumptions and socializations—a world that more and more will see through us. We risk being labeled as out of date, insecure, and complaining males who make excuses for shortcomings and behavior.

Yoho was challenging an old paradigm that used to work but no longer does. Men used to just be able to say, "Oh, I have a wife and kids," to get that pass. People like Ocasio-Cortez are helping to change the narrative around what it means to be held accountable for sexist words. As White men, it behooves us to get on board with the change that's happening, realize what side of history we want to be on, and be proactive rather than lamenting what is happening in the world and finding ourselves increasingly isolated and on the outs.

And we can also work with our own reactions to how events unfolded. Did we feel sorry for Yoho? Did we feel annoyed at Representative Ocasio-Cortez? Did we miss our opportunity to consider how strange it is that White men are so used to being comfortable that women and Black and brown people are considered perpetrators if they don't cater to that sense of privilege? And if we did consider that, did shame rise up? If you did feel shame, did some part of you try to project it away and into the world of those who reminded you of our history? Did it feel like others or the news cycle generated your shame like the proverbial maggots just showing up on meat?

Shame can knock us off balance, undermining our sense of agency. And it does so without ever announcing itself. This invisibility of shame makes it potentially even more damaging. We ought not talk or text or write or react when we're in shame. We've got to go inward to get ourselves and our nervous systems back in working order and out of the traumatic state that shame induces. Only when we've gotten enough clarity to regain our equilibrium can we go back out into the world.

Shame can be a doorway for positive change, and an opportunity for growth and self-respect. When we dive into it, we are reminded of our need to be humble and tender toward ourselves, to have compassion. Instead of snapping back to the status quo, we can come out the other side with a deeper sense of our own and others' humanity. I'm often reminded of the power of loving myself and being grounded in something other than the mistake I made. It allows me to reconnect with the part of me that is not the behavior. I gain a deeper connection with myself. My real self, the authentic core of me that is inherently worthy.

Shame often partners with feelings of unworthiness. When we seek status through income and career, our achievements can act as a way of warding off unworthiness. We feel superior when we feel we're doing better than others. Over time, this so-called superiority turns hollow, though. A financial advisor friend once had her clients set goals and target their ideal annual returns. What she discovered over time was that the closer those people came to reaching their goal, the more anxious and dissatisfied they grew. Their financial success wasn't bringing the feelings of accomplishment and security and confidence they expected.

There will always be someone who seems to have more than we do. We must evaluate our feelings of superiority and inferiority to realize that they exist right next to one another and that shame underlies them both. Though we won't always want to, we must lean in.

PUSH PAST STIGMA

Another potent dynamic standing in the way of leaning into our feelings is stigma. Therapist Lori Gottlieb puts it this way: "No matter how open we as a society are about formerly private matters, the stigma around our emotional struggles remains formidable. We'll talk with almost anyone about our physical health, even our sex lives, but bring up anxiety or loneliness or an intractable sense of grief, and the expression on the face looking back at you will probably read, "Get me out of this conversation, pronto."

Certainly, we men do this to one another. Sometimes, women also unknowingly reinforce the stigma for us by saying things like "Oh, don't get all philosophical on me" when we try to share what we feel, or, "I need you to be strong for me, because I'm getting emotional right now."

A friend once told me about walking home past a fraternity house in a college town and seeing a guy sitting on a curb, crying openly. She rushed over and asked him what was wrong. He told her he had just graduated, and had majored in something he hated, a degree his father had pushed him to get. He was crying because now he knew he would have to go work at a job he hated. He was drunk and that had let all this sorrow and regret burst forth. Here was a young man with everything ahead, regretting not his past, but his future to come.

It's one of the costs of our White male socialization: we don't end up knowing, wanting, or even caring what our heart really desires because we're too busy following the White male path set out for us, especially the need to make money and be considered successful according to societal standards that don't take our feelings into account. Men have been trained to ask themselves, "How much money is that going to bring me?" instead of the important question, "What does my heart want and what do I really care about?"

Like my headmaster sweeping aside our feelings of homesickness, we as White men are constantly socialized to ignore our feelings. Feelings are stigmatized as something allowed to women who, according to our socialization, are "less than." We men, meanwhile, have to be above feelings, repressing and marginalizing them, to exercise self-control. But you're not actually exercising self-control, just denial.

If we want to live the life we want, we have to push back against the stigma emotions carry so that we become better at handling ourselves. If we don't, feelings become a liability, harming us and bursting out in the one socially acceptable emotion for men: anger. That often later turns into rage or resentment or sobbing in great regret on a frat house curbside because you put your heart last.

KEYSTONE EMOTIONS

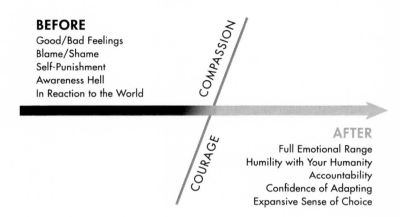

BEFORE
Good/Bad Feelings
Blame/Shame
Self-Punishment
Awareness Hell
In Reaction to the World

COMPASSION

COURAGE

AFTER
Full Emotional Range
Humility with Your Humanity
Accountability
Confidence of Adapting
Expansive Sense of Choice

Although all emotions have value, two in particular are extremely important. I've dubbed them "Keystone Emotions." A keystone is a stone in an arch without which the arch would fall. I had known for years about Robert Paine, the professor of zoology at the University of Washington in Seattle who coined the term keystone species. As an ecologist, Paine conducted an experiment to see if and how certain species hold more ecological influence than others. He laid out two areas on the Washington coastline teeming with diverse ocean life. Paine removed starfish from one of them. After a few weeks, the area without the starfish had dwindled down to just mussels. Without starfish, the mussel population took over everything, and the diversity of life that was once there disappeared. The starfish were the area's keystone species, a species upon which the rest of the ecosystem depends for healthy diversity. In writing this book, Paine's work came back to me, and I realized that our human emotional ecosystem requires two keystone emotions: courage and compassion. They are critical, powerful, necessary emotions that we must actively cultivate to create a healthy internal life.

Courage has traditionally been associated with masculinity—you know, charge into harrowing situations and show the boldness of courage. Compassion has been traditionally labeled as feminine and is associated with gentleness, love, and nurturing. When we meet all of our other feelings with courage and compassion, we cultivate a rich, nuanced emotional landscape that creates a powerful agility. Think of courage as a gas pedal that takes us forward into life with all its challenges. Compassion is the brake that helps us slow down around the corners that require more attention and a slower speed. You have both pedals at your disposal during any moment in life. We will often need to step on the gas pedal of courage to get going, navigate a hill, or go into uncomfortable parts. And yet we will also, just as importantly, use the brake pedal to maneuver the twists and turns or stop signs that life invariably presents.

Courage allows us to feel a greater range of things because we find it within ourselves to tolerate more than "good or bad" emotions. As Maya Angelou put it, "Without courage, we cannot practice any other virtue with consistency. We can't be kind, true, merciful, generous, or honest."

Courage lets us tolerate uncertainty, too—the discomfort, confusion, and awkwardness we experience when feelings do not resolve themselves quickly. These include feelings arising from the issues that challenge our culture, complex issues such as systemic racism and sexism.

Courage also helps us make it through unfulfilling or upsetting times in our relationships, times when there may be no apparent and quick reward for our efforts. The need to delay our rewards is important to relationships like marriage and close friendships. After all, the seeds of these relationships, these issues, these feelings, don't grow in a day: they have to be planted in soil, watered, exposed to sunlight. We have to keep having the courage to stay with these relationships and have tough conversations, even when they don't always yield the immediate results we want.

Compassion, meanwhile, helps us make space for everything we feel. It helps us refrain from incessantly judging our feelings or moving too quickly through them. Yes, it can give us empathy for others, but its greater importance is when it is focused on ourselves. If we don't understand what we're feeling and needing, we tend to look for the outside world to fill our unmet needs and affirm our worthiness. But that affirmation is not the responsibility of others: it's ours, and self-compassion helps us shoulder it.

Self-compassion allows for our own feelings and lets us patiently understand ourselves and connect with our worthiness. We can then interact with others without expecting them to fill our own needs.

Even better, as the ancient Chinese philosopher Lao Tzu once said: "Being loved gives you strength. Loving others gives you courage." Courage and compassion go hand in hand.

Compassion is often a tough sell for men. It gets tangled up in the stigma of feelings we discussed earlier. Men often think that if they display self-compassion, they are weak. Or that they are soft. They equate compassion with a lack of accountability as if showing compassion to others or self is akin to giving a pass on taking responsibility for failings.

On the contrary: I would argue that true compassion is actually deep accountability because it acknowledges, with tenderness and forgiveness, that something painful happened. When you are compassionate toward yourself, you are holding yourself accountable, because you know there's something greater. You know you can do better.

When I lead clients through the emotional work of privilege, I start by bringing up a kind of trigger, something having to do with race or sex or gender. They might be confused or overwhelmed or angry or uneasy at rioting, for example. I then instruct my clients to meet those feelings with courage and compassion, so that they can continue to deepen their connection to the challenging triggered emotions.

Even when they devolve into despair, shame, or any other kind of deep, dark emotions these triggers can evoke, I ask them to lean on courage and compassion. Instead of following an urge to act on the trigger, I invite them to accept and observe the feelings. To bring in additional information to add context to the trigger. Then the understanding of the situation and events begins to change. The trigger is the chance to see beneath the first emotional reactions, and to see the world in a broader and new way.

Only by doing this can we begin to ask the questions of grappling: "Why is this important to me? What does this mean about and for me? Who am I in this?" The process helps them turn toward their values in the middle of these difficult emotions. It helps them connect to who they are and what they stand for. Then they can ask themselves: what does authentic action look like from this place?

Back to the metaphor of the keystone species, the area devoid of the starfish. When we take away the feelings of compassion and courage, we are left with a reduced, less healthy emotional world. Psychologist Linda Graham calls it an emotional world of BASHing: Blame, Anger, Shame, and Helplessness become bad habits we can't get out of, loops of behavior that do not serve us.

Sometimes, when I see these clients start to really hurt, I'll give them a high five or a fist bump, as a way of sort of saying, "You got this. You can do this." I want this masculine response to show them the real value of their work: This is how men become heroes, true badasses—by engaging in a wrestling match with their emotions. What bigger, more beautiful, powerful, courageous thing could you do than look your own demons and monsters straight in the eyes?

Let's take a moment to talk about stress and burnout. Referring to job burnout specifically, the University of California dubbed it the billion-dollar problem because of the low energy, chronic feelings of exhaustion and stress that won't go away, stress and burnout that takes a toll on workers and on companies. It's a kind of cynicism towards career and even life, that leaves people feeling powerless and without tools to change.

The good news is that the sustained effort of grappling can overturn this widespread phenomenon and offset the "burnout culture" that is rampant and sweeping workplaces. As a power broker and leader in your life, you can have a direct effect on your workplace culture, while failure to grapple can ripple out, causing a decline in morale, wellness, and productivity.

HOW TO START

Just as with the grappling move of learning, I recommend you start with the keystone emotion that is your strength. If you're good at having compassion for your children, you may more easily make the connection between your heart toward your kids and your heart toward yourself. Or if you've had to have courage at times in your life, then you can channel this toward your emotions. The point to remember is, if you've ever acted courageous once, if you've ever acted compassionately once, you know how to do it. It may be a challenge to apply it to a new situation, but you can do it. You've proven you have the capacity.

I've worked with extreme athletes who show great courage skiing off cliffs or jumping out of planes. I try to help them channel that same courage into helping them deal with their emotions. The challenge I run into is that many of these athletes actually shut down their emotions so they can cope with the challenge of these extreme sports. Emotions are the last thing they want to feel. But I want to show them how these are actually good training for jumping off the emotional cliffs in their lives.

Wherever you join this journey—whether it's in your relationships, within yourself, or as part of societal change—your strengths can help. You can go in and navigate the familiar territory until you get to the end of what you know, then going a little further and taking a few more steps into the unknown. Come out, then, get some relief, and go back in a little farther the next time.

While this is going on, you'll have to push "pause" on your need for action, your instinct to try to fix or solve everything.

You'll have to allow yourself the experience of feeling for the sake of learning and understanding, and for gaining a measure of comfort in the discomfort of emotions, especially at the beginning of your emotional journey. You must allow yourself to feel—not instantly reject feelings—no matter how strange or uncomfortable it feels. Compassion provides the space to feel without self-judgment.

Kristin Neff has spent her entire career studying self-compassion. Her work shows that when we invite compassion in we can see the "common humanity" that connects us to the world and its people. That sense that we all experience some version of what is happening in this moment can be powerful to cultivate. It can energize us to keep moving forward in life.

And you must think about how you feel about feeling, to build a bridge between your mind and your heart. We must start to build a vocabulary beyond feelings as good or bad. You're learning the language in the previously foreign land of your heart. Being able to name new landmarks will start to make it feel like home.

It is home. It is you.

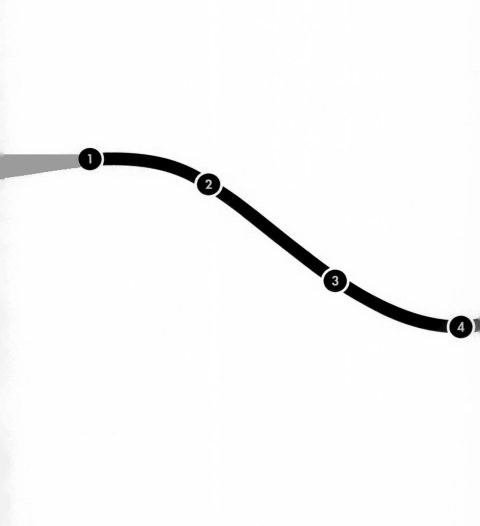

GRAPPLING 101

"When you come to the end of all the light you know, and it's time to step into the darkness of the unknown, faith is knowing that one of two things shall happen: Either you will be given something solid to stand on or you will be taught to fly."
—Edward Teller

I want to share a story about humiliation, redemption, and the opportunities of grappling. It features a guy I know who wanted to build a basketball court for his son, so he tore down a shed that was in the way.

This was no everyday shed. It was a historic shed, on a property that sat in a national historic district. When the guy bought his property, he knew that he could not take down this shed, at least not without approval from a historic board. But he couldn't figure out where else he would build a basketball court. When he mentioned the possibility of demolishing the shed to his wife, she said, "I don't think it's a good idea."

Impulsively, the guy decided to do it anyway. The shed sat behind his house, on his property, after all, and if he wanted to build a basketball court, he should damn well be able to do so. He told his contractor to rip the shed down (the contractor also expressing reservations), and immediately started building a basketball court. He doubted there would be any ramifications.

Well, months after the court was finished, someone tipped off the city, and the guy was busted. He spent the next five months dealing with mounting problems. First, he had to hire a lawyer. He had to write letters to city officials to explain why he flouted the historic laws, and to build his case for keeping his son's court. He had to convince neighbors to support his case. He and his wife had to speak before the historic board, then speak before the city council.

Their appearance at the council meeting was streamed live on the city's TV station, on the internet and viewed all over the city. The couple spoke, answered questions, and expressed regret about their mistake, but still the guy didn't believe anything would actually happen to them. What could the council members do, tell him to rebuild the shed?

To his shock, that was exactly what happened. After the guy and his wife spoke before the council, the city council members voted 8-0 to order the couple to tear down the brand-new basketball court and rebuild the shed to historic standards. One member even shook her head at them and called them "you people."

The guy was dumbfounded. "Are you kidding me?" he asked over and over. He left the meeting feeling defeated. But it would get worse.

The next morning, he walked out to his driveway to pick up the local newspaper, a ritual he loved, fetching the paper and reading it over coffee. He always looked forward to it. And after the night before, he needed it. He fetched his paper and his heart stopped: he and his shed were the lead story on the front page.

It didn't stop there: his tale of humiliation ended up being reported all over the state. Meanwhile, the guy had to spend tens of thousands of dollars to hire contractors to jackhammer and tear up the basketball court. He had to hire architects to re-envision what the historic shed looked like in its heyday, and then he had to search for the materials that would have been used at that time. And remember how the guy's wife had told him not to do this? She eventually sat him down and said: "This was not okay. I can't believe you did this to me. I told you not to do it, and I feel violated."

By now you're probably thinking that guy is a real asshole, or at least a total amateur who needs to learn how to grapple. You're thinking this is a textbook case of an entitled White man who doesn't think through his decisions or recognize how they impact others.

The asshole is me. Yes, me, who makes a living teaching others about grappling and respecting the feelings of others.

Even though I knew better, even though I had spent years contemplating and reckoning and grappling with my privilege and my impulsiveness, I still made a rogue decision. I wanted what I wanted, and I didn't think there would be any real penalty. I turned deaf to the tiny voice in me that knew I shouldn't do it, even if I could do it and get away with it.

But I didn't get away with it. Instead, I felt waves of shame and waves of accountability. First when I was caught violating the historic standards, then when the city council ordered us to rebuild the shed, and then walking out to pick up the morning paper only to see our shame splashed onto the front page. And to this day, it still comes up randomly. And each time, I still cringe.

Faced with condemnation all around, I felt immature and irresponsible. The situation brought me back to my past, to that feeling of being a screwup, of being powerless. But now I was no longer a child. I had the capacity to grapple, even though I couldn't rectify my mistake.

Over the next several weeks, I played the entire episode consciously and unconsciously in my mind. I went back in time, I rewound the clock, and I asked myself, what was I thinking in that moment that I chose to tear down the shed? What was I feeling? What was happening in my body at that moment, and before that moment, and after that moment? What were the circumstances under which I made such a rash decision?

Gradually and after a lot of grappling, I discovered a number of reasons. At the core was my old impulsivity, combined with a sense of impunity and plenty of entitlement. Much of it was also unconscious and internalized privilege that stemmed from being a straight White man and the socialization that told me I could do whatever I wanted in my domain.

I also realized that previous to me tearing down the shed, my wife and I had undertaken interior renovations in our house, during which I found her decision-making process too deliberate and overly meticulous. I was irritated by my role as bystander in the renovations, simply watching my wife as the main decision-maker. I felt powerless.

Now I see things in a different context than I did at the time. Grappling after the fact, I can see there were a million red flags. Warning lights, stop signs, yellow lights, flashing red lights—I blew through them all. I ignored the part of me that cares about my community and my responsibilities, in favor of my reactionary side, my White privilege, and my sense of ownership of my family and private property. It was bitter medicine to swallow, but discerning what the learning is, owning the hard lessons, these are fundamental to grappling.

Learning my lesson was hard. While I was experiencing those waves of shame and humiliation, I was at the mercy of others, giving my power away. Others had written the story of this imbroglio: The neighbor who told on me. The newspaper. My wife. The city council. The Denver TV station who picked it up and spread my mistake even farther afield.

But there was a missing writer: me. I was a victim of the narrative up until the moment I said, "No more. I've got to take this story back. I need to go inward and figure out for me what the hell happened." Because clearly there was a cognitive dissonance between how I saw myself and how I showed up in the world.

I began the process of owning my story by rewriting it to include the context of my life at the time, and what had been going on in my head and heart, the main settings of the story. I began accepting the consequences I will always have to bear, including occasional shocks where others recognize me by it—"Oh, that was *you* who tore down the shed!"

It's always humbling and a reminder to cultivate self-compassion. Grappling has given me this, this reminder to be no bigger than myself and no smaller than myself, to carry humility with my humanity. We're always there for ourselves when things go great. We owe it to ourselves to be there all the time, be there for our full humanity, especially when things go south.

But my story is mine now. I am transparent about it when it comes up. Of course, it still hurts a bit, but that's slowly going away because I always have access to the tenderness that is there inside of me. I can call on that tenderness to wash over the part of me that made the mistake. The place where self-compassion meets mistake is the birthplace of self-forgiveness for my past and the beginning of a more authentic future.

Grappling is a choice to rise to the occasion in the context of where you are right now. It is a deliberate process that places you in the thick of the challenges and opportunities of the moment. Remember that grappling is engaging in a close struggle without weapons. It takes the strength of courage but also the strength of compassion, no weapons, against its growing pains. It requires kindness, self-compassion, and tenderness for mistakes, old wounds, and destructive patterns.

But again, it is a choice. First, recognize when you need to grapple, and then commit to it.

THE FOUR STAGES OF GRAPPLING

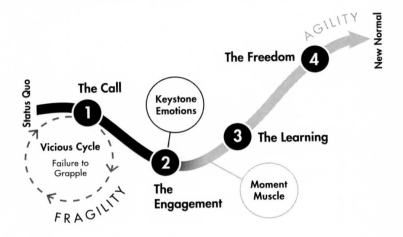

1. **The Call.** The call could be a feeling inside that we are finally ready to deal with. It could be an external stimulus like a wife asking for a divorce. It might be a gnawing discomfort while viewing police brutality. Whatever it is, we begin to grapple when we turn towards it and say, "Okay, enough. I'm ready. Let's do this. I don't want to look away any longer. If this is something I learned and it's not me at my core, well then, I can unlearn it. It's the step where you roll up the sleeves, which is so necessary for grappling. In this first part, we need to get beyond ourselves and connect with others to fortify for the journey by way of the community around us. Get out of the silo that

is our emotional experience. You might talk to friends, a mentor, read a book by a respected expert—just reach beyond yourself. Answer the call.

2. **The Engagement.** Engaging means being willing to get uncomfortable, to go deeper towards uncertainty and to let go of what we thought was true. During this stage, we acquire more information about ourselves and the world around us, but we can't quite make sense of it yet. We are keeping our foot on the pedal of courage to see things we previously weren't ready to see and braking with the pedal of compassion when necessary to breathe when things get too hard or aren't making sense. We reach out for support and share our journey. Even though we lack clarity, letting others in empowers us to move forward in this messy middle. The struggle is hard, and that invites our conscious engagement.

3. **The Learning.** In this phase, we are loving the learning! Life is a practice, and we are stepping away from having to know, instead leaning into the learning and connecting the dots in our lives. There is a through line, and our grappling muscle is becoming stronger as it starts to comprehend life and ourselves on a deeper level. We now choose to move towards

even more unresolved things in our lives because we have experienced the success and the clarity that grappling brings. Learning feels good!

4. **The Freedom.** No longer a conscious thing, grappling is how we live. It's fundamental to how we show up to life. And it brings a level of liberation that is generative. We are agents of change, not because we have power over others but because of the power inside us. We have more energy than ever before. Our life becomes a kind of creative expression: we are the canvas on which our life gets created. As we move into this phase, our authenticity and our lives become an act of service, less about us in an egoistic way. This is an act of letting go over and over again, one that begets a freedom we never experienced before as we rewrite the past, present, and future.

WHEN YOU NEED TO GRAPPLE

There are two major signs that you need to grapple:

- **Sign Number One:** When you realize on your own that you can show up better in life. You have a strong intention for what you want out of life. You have a sense of possibility, something better.

You realize that you're learning and growing. You decide to listen to your feelings and allow them to inform you of something. You decide to be open to the possibilities that life is offering you. And you deliberately set a proactive mindset that says, "Whatever's happening, I'm going to learn, I'm going to rewrite this story to make it rich and full, and I am going to seek more."

- **Sign Number Two:** You have a sense of the cost of what is happening in your life. Things aren't going well and you courageously look that cost directly in the eye. For example, a crisis or instigating event occurs; for instance, me realizing I had to drop out of college, or picking up the paper and seeing my failings broadcast on the front page.

Number two comes with warning signs. You are irritated or frustrated with other people. You might feel resistant or angry because of the situation, and you'd like to project these feelings onto someone else. You may feel as if you are stuck, as if you don't have any choices, as if the odds are stacked against you. Or that something is happening to you.

When those things happen, you're not necessarily going to have your sleeves rolled up, ready to rock and roll and do this grappling thing like you are when you get sign number one. You may be so busy putting out your own fires that you may not notice the need to grapple until months or even years later. The crisis might be taking all your available energy to manage staying afloat.

The good news is that grappling can turn you into a time-traveler. While you can't change the past, you can grapple to rewrite the past to reflect a truer, more complete picture. You can also open more fully to your present to reflect your inner reality right now. And you can reimagine the story of your future. What is possible feels so much more expansive from this place.

Let's go through all three of these time-traveling grappling modes.

GRAPPLING WITH THE PAST

William Faulkner once said, "The past is never dead. It's not even past."

Reaching into the past sometimes requires a bit of pre-grappling, setting the table for grappling. You can do this by reminding yourself, "This is not about me. I'm a good person." Connect with your aspirational self, the type of person you want to be. This will allow you to lean in and say, "I made a mistake. I missed something. I'm not seeing something I overlooked. I'm trying to *get it* right. Not *be* right."

Also use the tactic of moving your body and spending time in nature. When I go for a long walk in the woods and really think about things past (or present), looking at things from all angles and trusting myself, movement and nature help with my self-examination. Grappling doesn't have to be a solely intellectual exercise. Engaging our full beings helps awaken us. The wisdom of nature grounds us, helping us to grapple. Moving your body helps you navigate the rough spots. The wisdom traditions can be a powerful source as well. The Asaro Tribe has a saying that, "Knowledge is only rumor until it lives in the bones." Biking with my brother helped me grapple after dropping out of college with those long stretches of rhythmic movement. I pedaled my way all the way back to myself.

The basketball court is another physical manifestation of how I learned one of my most powerful grappling techniques, which I call "go slow to go fast." As a former basketball coach, I've used this technique with my players. We teach basketball moves by slowing down to a step-by-step process. As coaches, we would demonstrate in slow motion, breaking things down in clear, slow steps. "First, you move this foot here. Then you bring the ball up with your right hand. At the same time, you rotate your body."

This can feel a bit laborious and trivial in the moment, but it proves crucial on the basketball court. It helped us nail the fundamentals first, before we began to speed up the move, repeating it over and over, getting better and better, until the point where we could do the moves quickly at game speed with a competitor in our face.

You can do this with your past. Slow down. Replay each event. Look at past situations where you didn't handle yourself in the way that you would have liked, or where the situation went wrong even though you didn't think you did anything wrong. Look for opportunities to zero in on details. Ask yourself what you were feeling. What opportunities you missed. What was happening inside you, and around you. Ask yourself how you reacted: did you ignore, deny, minimize, rationalize, avoid—all of those non-grappling maneuvers that are so easy to engage in? And did you bring the compassion you have for someone who is learning something new?

Think also about the precipitating events. Part of learning is zeroing in on that uncomfortable place right *before* something tipped the balance. That's the place where you can learn something new. So, rewind the tape back, re-experiencing that uncomfortable feeling of not knowing, and then look at what new information is there for you.

When I'm grappling with a previous mistake, I can likewise rewind the tape back to that period of time prior to the mistake and say, okay, what was happening? What was going on? How was I reacting? Then I evaluate what I could have done instead to make the situation turn out better. I wonder: how can I reimagine this situation in the context of the person I want to be? I envision what I wish I had done. It's a kind of do-over in my mind. It's a practice for similar situations in the future. Practicing being a better person in your heart and mind trains you to perform that way in your outer life.

It's important to deliberately wire in the positive alternative; otherwise, an innate negativity bias (e.g., "Why is it up to me to try so hard?") will rear its head. Research shows we can actually rewire our brains and their neural pathways. Doing all this work will speed up your grappling in the present and future. Situations will seem familiar because you have practiced them. You'll be able to more easily act in ways that align with the person you want to be. By writing a new past where you have figured out what your integrity should have done, you have scripted a better you in the present. This is, after all, a kind of reckoning about who we are in the world and the choices we want to make and the ways we can hold ourselves accountable. The time you spend reimagining the past builds agility for future situations. And your brain, when faced with a decision in the moment, feels as if it has already stepped onto the path of your better self, already made that decision the right way, the way you wanted.

Many people don't get beyond this first step of grappling with the past. My father doesn't always agree with me on this one. I have been trying to invite him to reflect on his childhood, particularly on his father's drinking. I wondered if he'd want to gain some deeper understanding into his life, maybe even do some rewriting. His response: "I don't understand why you have to bring this stuff up. It's the past. It's gone."

Maybe this is part of what happens when you get older. You'd like to die with the story you've learned to live with whether it hides important elements or not, whether it's harmful to deeper meaning or not. We choose the story we know even if it has its limitations. The known misery gets chosen over the unknown.

I understand that, but for me, this process is worth it. It's worth it to take on the past and parse it to look for indications of missed information. I wouldn't, for instance, have realized that my power play with the shed debacle actually spoke to feelings of powerlessness.

It is humbling to hold yourself accountable for previous mistakes, to speak them out loud instead of just silently listening to the nagging voice inside your head. But you will find it worth it because acknowledging that mistakes happened minimizes the internal impact on you. As Oprah Winfrey said, "I say the universe speaks to us, always, first in whispers. And a whisper in your life usually feels like, 'Hmm, that's odd.' Or, 'Hmm, that doesn't make any sense.' Or, 'Hmm, is that right?' It's that subtle. And if you don't pay attention to the whisper, it gets louder and louder and louder. I say it's like getting thumped upside the head. If you don't pay attention to that, it's like getting a brick upside your head."

We need to listen to these whispers. Our intuition speaks in a kind of whisper but gets louder and louder when we don't listen. And it's not a good idea not to listen. Just ask the guy who ripped down an historical shed.

He's the same guy that let his needs drown out consideration and respect for an ex-girlfriend, hurting her in the process. I was nineteen back in the late 1980s, single after a recent breakup. One night, my ex-girlfriend and I got together to talk. As we hung out talking during the evening, the possibility of us having sex seemed just like something we would fall back into as when we were together. But she didn't want to. She said no. I persisted. I wanted sex; that's what was ruling me. I kept cajoling and pressuring and eventually, she gave in against her better judgment. We went further than she wanted to.

A few months later, she came to me and said she needed to talk. She told me what happened from her perspective and teared up while sharing her pain. I felt terrible. I couldn't sweep her feelings under the rug or rationalize or marginalize them. I had done something wrong.

I apologized profusely, saying I understood my actions were not okay. She appreciated the apology. I was proud of myself in that moment and felt no lingering shame.

Fast forward years later to the #MeToo movement that started in 2017. I listened with horror to the stories of treatment women have to endure. I also heard something different I hadn't heard before. That they feel shame for not being able to say no, even though saying no in general is something socialization hasn't supported in women. I was struck by this fact. Women blame themselves for not being able to stand up for themselves the way they wanted. It's like they punish themselves and declare war on their self-esteem. My nineteen-year-old behavior crept back into my mind.

I thought about the power of the sexual urge for men and how problematic that was. I had given into that urge, disrespecting my ex-girlfriend's wishes. Governed by those urges, I didn't bother to think about deferring to her. If someone had pointed out the misogyny in what I was doing, I would have been shocked. But I wasn't being true with myself. I was busy trying to take something from her.

I found my ex-girlfriend's number and called her. We had talked a few times in the ensuing years, but the call still came as a surprise to her. I told her that the #MeToo movement had taught me a lot, and I wanted to again say I was sorry. I had learned so much about the impact of my actions. I made a mistake, it wasn't okay, and she didn't deserve that treatment.

It was humbling to grapple with my behavior on the phone with her, but it had to be done. It was right to give her the chance to hold me accountable. It strengthened us both. She appreciated the call.

I've also spoken to my teenage son multiple times about these situations and emphasized the mutuality of sexual encounters, the importance of respecting no, the need to be careful and proceed with respect.

This whole process does make us stronger, maybe especially when we are on our knees, making ourselves vulnerable. I let in more pain and vulnerability by evaluating what I had done in the context of #MeToo, and by calling my ex to apologize once again. But now I don't have to hide or feel ashamed. Coming to terms with what I'd done and how I'd made someone else feel liberated me—not because I got off the hook but because I got in touch with more of my power and strength, my humanity and humility, and, most of all, my agency.

I demonstrated to myself that I can show up in the world even as an imperfect man understanding I'm still a good human being who made a terrible mistake. I'm not hiding pieces of myself in a closet under lock and key, becoming less whole, as a result.

Wholeness is no joke. It's fundamental to who we are, to how we show up. When we split ourselves into pieces, fragmenting our being, it doesn't just damage ourselves.

Abusing and assailing our wholeness means we can perpetrate anything on society: if we are callous toward ourselves, we will be callous toward others.

We have a problem with dehumanizing others in our society that can stem directly from this dehumanizing of our wholeness.

GRAPPLING IN THE PRESENT

When you are ready, as Edward Teller said, to step into the darkness of the unknown and grapple in the present, keep a few things in mind.

Grappling isn't a one-time thing, a one-shot deal, like you read this book and then boom, you can always grapple perfectly. Grappling is a way of life. Musicians never stop practicing scales or exercises. Athletes never stop training. Good teachers never stop learning. We all have to practice our skills to keep them in good working order. And the chance of backsliding is always there given how entwined our socialization is with our deepest beings. Even after years of this work, I still allowed my socialized ego to kick in and tear down the shed. Back to Grappling 101.

First, remember to use the grappling moves of learning and feeling. Regard these as lifelong tools to be used together when you grapple in the present. As we discussed in Chapter 4, emotions are important to learning. They can help us more easily assimilate new information. We can manifest new external landscapes in our path in life, if we have a sense of our own internal emotional landscape. My learning was only able to take off after I dropped out of college and spent three years biking, reflecting, rewriting, practicing. Once you begin grappling, you may see your cognitive and physical abilities take off, as well. That increases your real-time agility, to grapple even as a challenging situation unfolds.

When I was a high school basketball coach in my thirties, my team faced a discouraging halftime break. The other team was employing a full-court defense after each score, turning the ball over for a quick layup and rattling my kids. I had tried to review my strategies from the sidelines, but they didn't seem to be registering with the kids. In the locker room, I could explain yet another way to try to break the other team's press. Or I could help my team grapple.

I began asking each player what he felt and got the responses I expected: "angry," "overwhelmed," "panicky," "nervous." One said: "I'm worried about turning the ball over. I start to get pissed at myself and then I rip other teammates."

I told them, "Yes, you're playing basketball and dribbling and shooting and defending, but you're also managing your internal experience, your internal emotions as you're playing the game. It's a parallel process." The team nodded in understanding. They got it. They'd just been living that process for a grueling first half.

As we left the locker room to return to the game, we walked past a bunch of older coaches laughing in their office. "Hey, Horning, come here," they said, snickering. "Did you say, 'Manage your internal experience emotionally?' Bah!" These coaches were good guys, but emotions were a foreign concept to them. They did not understand what I was saying nearly as well as my team did.

What happened next? My team ended up breaking the press and winning the game. Strategy had never been the issue: we had practiced this press break before, and they knew it well. The issue was that my kids were overstimulated and couldn't navigate their emotions enough to execute the strategy.

I never went back to the old coaches and said "Hey, look what worked!" But it had. The kids felt, they learned, they learned to manage what they felt. They used the grappling hooks and it carried them over the wall they'd been hitting, all the way up to victory.

As I've mentioned, my journey has not been about struggling to express emotions as it is for many men, but instead about learning how to appropriately contain them. So, when I told those players to manage their internal experience, I was speaking from a lifetime of managing my own emotions, a lifelong practice of learning the balance between expression and containment, and how doing this emotional management can raise your performance in all areas of your life. You might be shaky at first, but over time, you will learn this balance. You will increase your agility. You will be able to spot opportunities for grappling and respond from moment to moment, moving through the experience to the other side.

When I was growing up in Washington, D.C., my dad would drive us through Rock Creek Park, this beautiful ribbon of federal parkland that includes Rock Creek. In those days, to cross Rock Creek, you could drive over a bridge, or you could also occasionally ford it. The officials would open the ford crossing and our car could cross right through the creek.

As a six-year-old, that drop into the creek was scary and wonderful. We'd stick our heads out of the windows and look down, water rising up the tires, and in a moment of panic, wonder, "Oh, god! Is the water going to come in the car? Are we going to get swept down the creek?" Fortunately, though, the car would keep going forward and eventually reach the other side. We would rise up the embankment feeling the exhilaration, wanting to do it all over again.

Too often people start to ford their feelings, but when they get too deep for comfort, they retreat back to the safety of known shores. People often think of feelings as a bottomless pit to be afraid of. But feelings do have a ground.

You can get to the other side of them. There is traction, a creek bed and road up and out. A road to the other side.

Others are afraid they'll get swept away by their feelings, but the way you get swept away is by standing still instead of moving through. If this is difficult, even traumatic, find allies in your grappling, or seek out professional help. Some people have put traumatic feelings away for so long, the support is necessary. You don't have to fall into the memory of a trauma and live it all over again. Have someone there as you ford your feelings. This is difficult. But remember that you don't have to do it by yourself; you are not alone.

Mainly, know that this journey is worth it. Yes, it can be scary, this going down into waters where the bottom isn't clear. And we're used to that good/bad feeling construct so the first sign of discomfort and fear sends many of us back the direction we came. If that sounds like you, wouldn't you like to know what it would be like to stay with your feelings until you reached the other side? To know depth of them for the sake of a profound transformational experience?

Instead, we build a bridge or dam the creek or build tunnels or fly planes to avoid the experience of dipping our toes in the waters. It might appear more convenient and even initially seem to be the easier of the two choices, but it's not the way to accrue the experiences that help us learn what we're made of.

The Moment Muscle

In the last chapter, I mentioned the "moment muscle"—that is, developing the strength to stay in the moment. To help build this muscle, learn to regard feelings as a learning opportunity. (Remember, learning and feeling are connected.) In the moment, lean into what you're feeling, despite discomfort, in order to get the lay of it. Engage the feeling—move toward it, not away from it. Shying away just lays the groundwork for defensiveness and rationalization, strong barriers to your growth.

Moment muscle is when you take the opportunity that this moment offers and view it as a gift. Engaging with the moment adds deep presence to it, complete with all the senses you can experience that you otherwise wouldn't. But it does take practice and you should view it as such. The more you do it, the better you become at it, so practice it on a daily basis. You could practice during conversations with your children as you slow down to listen. You could practice when you're eating food, slowing down to taste, smell, live in the visceral experience of it.

Most of all, practice developing a moment muscle around what you are feeling. Is it the desire to please? A desire to connect? Loneliness? Awkwardness? From those identified feelings, you can glean what you need.

Research shows that loneliness is the last taboo emotion. We will admit we are anxious or depressed much more quickly than we will ever acknowledge to ourselves or to others that we are lonely. And awkward also gets shoved aside. Mostly because we are socialized to try to be chill, even if "chill" is just a phrase we've learned to utter. It can feel counterintuitive that allowing for moments of loneliness or celebrating moments of awkwardness develops agility more quickly. The simple acknowledgment often acts as a tipping point and can have the impact of making you less lonely and less awkward.

The moment muscle that slows us down to ground us in the present gives us the chance to choose to notice and move toward a feeling. Feelings can happen internally while we choose an expression externally. So the agility comes from knowing the feeling and intentionally choosing how to act from that feeling.

That can, though, be overwhelming at first, so start small. I used to practice using my moment muscle at stoplights when I was stressed and anxious and feeling powerless. I remember saying to myself while at a stoplight, "All right, I'm just going to bring kindness to everything I'm feeling. I'm just going to love myself and be compassionate with myself for all that is happening. And I'm going to do this until this light turns green: be gentle, tender, sweet, kind, compassionate, loving."

And by the time the light turned green, I'd feel a little better. The challenges were still there, but just practicing that moment muscle of self-compassion for a few seconds brought me so much more agility to face the day. I still had problems, but I was no longer mired in beating myself up or blaming myself or others for what I was feeling. Although blame can feel good initially, it leaves us stuck and unable to create the change the blame attempted to.

Mindfulness and meditation are popular tools to develop your moment muscle with the added benefit of programs that include guidance. And they're highly effective. Addiction psychiatrist Judson Brewer has found that mindfulness is actually five times more effective than other addiction or cessation programs. Five times!

When you practice mindfulness, you allow the moment to be what is. To do this, you also practice tolerance. If the moment involves your own feelings—feelings that might be unwelcome—you accept and greet the feelings with compassion. Mindfulness reduces resistance and feeds acceptance.

Another moment muscle strategy I learned from sports might resonate with those of you who are coaches and athletes: Don't play the scoreboard. Play the process.

When we play the scoreboard, we're focused on who's winning, which creates a bit of a disembodied experience. We're not centered on ourselves, living from that center. We're up there, laser-focused on the scoreboard. We miss a lot of what's going on around us as we start projecting ourselves into the future score on the board, and into the past, where the score used to be.

When we switch our mindset and play the process, we land in the moment of what we're doing. We double down on living out the present. Instead of saying, "I'm losing" or "I'm winning," we are in a moment of time where process means that winning or losing isn't relevant yet. Only when the process stops is the outcome determined.

Raising Your Frustration Tolerance

A key step in your ability to grapple in the present is developing a high tolerance for frustration. Frustrated people have two routes: try to shove frustration away in knee-jerk fashion (the LTF folks) or tolerate it (the HTF folks). Unlike those with low frustration-tolerance, people possessing high frustration-tolerance make situational observations and then choices. Understanding the sources of frustration can be so liberating. You begin to own it as you look for answers: Is the problem solvable or unsolvable? Will it be over quickly, or will it linger? You can put words to your feelings, ask for what you want, and deal with it in the moment. You can choose to leave the situation or find humor in the situation. In short, you have agency, and that foils frustration.

If you practice this process during enough small, less loaded moments, say, when you're watching the TV news or when you're driving, over time you will develop HFT and grow immensely in the process. An HFT allows you to say to yourself, "I'm frustrated by people right now. I know that means I need time alone." Or, "I'm hungry and getting grouchy with my clients. If I eat, I will feel more patient." If you remain a person with LFT— you can think back to the things you've done in the face of frustration. Cell phones thrown into overgrown fields, holes punched in walls, slammed doors, slammed fists on tables—even laying on the horn to drown out a six-year-old little girl. HFT gives you the ability to do something constructive with those frustrated feelings so that you have the sustained energy to keep moving forward and not stop in exhaustion, over-whelm, or burnout.

GRAPPLING IN THE FUTURE

Our goal is to be able to make choices in the future that better represent ourselves and our feelings. Here are some strategies you can use to do so:

Unfreeze, Change, Refreeze

"Unfreeze, change, refreeze" is German-American psychol-ogist Kurt Lewin's three-step model change theory. It involves unfreezing your behavior, thoughts or feelings, making changes, then refreezing the new behaviors, the new ways of being.

Of course, this is often done at a time of great upheaval. You know you have to unfreeze the status quo. When I picked up that newspaper and saw myself as the lead story, I knew that the previous order of my life was gone. This place is often referred to as the "messy middle." I wasn't sure what was falling into its place, but I did know my understanding of my own situation had fundamentally changed. The status quo was getting shaken up.

This unfreezing the status quo, changing it, then refreezing it takes time, but without it, the future is predetermined. Whether through upheaval or a gradual sense that things must change, unfreezing is your chance to change your own story. You can re-envision your future and freeze that into a new and better normal. Where before we might only see one option, now we may see many. We are rewiring our brain to allow for feeling, learning, and possibility.

Unanswered Questions

Early on in my journey, I came across Rainer Maria Rilke's beautiful quote: "Be patient toward all that is unsolved in your heart and try to love the questions themselves."

Unanswered questions tempt us to fall into the quick fix, quick answer habit. Instead of trying to solve for them, to fix them as you are socialized to do. Instead, sit a little longer in the limbo of the I don't know. There's untangling to do.

Yes, it feels counterintuitive, holding onto questions instead of grabbing for answers. But it's better to do something that may seem even more counterintuitive: find more questions, questions regarding your life.

Working to frame such questions is empowering because then you can live your answers. We are the canvas on which our life gets created. Ask yourself, "What is the question that my life is offering me now in this moment? What's the question that's unanswered?" Neuroscience has found that when we hold a question we don't know the answer to, our brain will go to work without us even trying, searching for the answer. In fact, your brain releases serotonin so you can relax.

I like to spend time with these questions in my own life. It helps me consider my own path and push out my growth edge. On a personal level, some of the questions I hold are, "How am I dealing with the impulsivity of my feelings?" and "What would it look like if I enhanced my leadership abilities?"

One aspect of my professional life is being in business with my family. My parents are aging, and my siblings and I have entered a new chapter of claiming our roles as the second generation in the business. My dad has provided us a lot of wisdom and gifts, as well as a legacy that is beautiful and powerful in some ways but unresolved in others. Our job is to inherit this legacy and move it one step forward. How will we do this?

These questions don't need to be answered immediately, and they can't be. I try and invite in and cultivate the patience that allows me to live into them and watch life reveal the answers as I continue questioning.

Hold your questions, tolerate frustration, use the past, the present, and possible futures to grapple and grow stronger. Make peace with yourself and let yourself be. That will provide more than enough inspiration and strength to step forward into the life you want.

THE GRAPPLING GAME PLAN

I've given you a lot of philosophy, but a theoretical approach only goes so far. We're switching to tactics now, a game plan for grappling. Using the word grapple as an acronym, each letter will represent a step or action to help you engage in a close struggle without weapons.

GRAPPLE:
- **G**rounding
- **R**eflection on "Why"
- **A**gility
- **P**ractice
- **P**aradox
- **L**earning
- **E**quity and Justice

Grounding

A good first step is to ground into our being, our core. We can invest in unconditional love toward ourselves and let that root us.

We're socialized to do and to have, but in reality, the most important thing is to *be*. Many men get lost in thinking they are what they do, rather than they do what they are. Which gives a circumstantial sense to our being. Truly grounding yourself is declaring that your life is not about circumstance, it's about who you are on the deepest level, regardless of the circumstances.

We're socialized to do things in order to have things. Money, job, relationship, house, vacation house—we keep piling on for status, believing that when we've "arrived" enough, we will be happy being.

Grappling proves that wrong. We discover that being takes precedence, and that what we do flows from that being. Having becomes the last priority and reflects what we have created on the inside.

Grounded in self, being and doing provides a life we want, our circumstances for good or bad only temporary. It's easier to be patient when we're never poor in spirit and heart. We are not our wounds nor our struggles. We are separate from whatever's happening in this moment, grounded in a deeper abiding permanence within us. When we ground in our core, we can be both the person that is struggling *and* the person who is providing nurturance and guidance to our experience. Both are possible.

Consider that at your core, there is a spirit, a light, an essence that is innately good. By grappling inward to discover your inner wisdom or deep knowing, you are doing the work of grounding. This is a kind of authenticity that will serve you well as life throws its challenges at you. Those who proclaim selflessness and don't meet their own needs end up unconsciously using others to meet their needs. There is such a thing as healthy-selfish. If we aren't selfish in the beginning, we end up being self-serving in the end.

Reflect on Why

This was a modality created by author and motivational speaker Simon Sinek, who says that everything is about the question "why?" Sinek recommends telling others your why, and engaging in a kind of reflection so you can consider what exactly your why is.

Another way to ask this why is to phrase it, "For the sake of what?" or even "What for?" I love this question because it speaks to purpose and can apply to everything. Coming at everything with curiosity and deep interest empowers us, preventing us from feeling fragile.

For instance, instead of just accepting things as they are, start to ask yourself, "For the sake of what am I doing this? Why am I spending my days the way I'm spending them?"

You could answer, "Well, to earn money," or "It's what the boss demands," or "I have to feed my family."

Then you can go deeper: "But what's my life purpose? Why am I choosing to spend the hours, minutes, weeks the way I am, and how is any of it related to purpose? Does it have to be this way, or do I want to do it differently?"

Maybe you're asking a different type of why—a question rather than a purpose. For example, perhaps you're struggling with: "Why do I have to watch every word I say around women?" You're not alone here. Many men feel frustrated. This why will take some exploration and reflection to feel more certainty about why and whether or not your words are appropriate or inappropriate. First identifying your deeper why here reinforces your willingness to explore the question itself. Your deeper "why," your purpose, may be the need to stay relevant, to not be left behind, to handle yourself when you interact with women. You want to feel secure instead of threatened when women are around, but you aren't sure how to avoid coming off as sexist and watching women cast cold looks at you, after which they think less of you. Losing the respect of women you need to get along with on a regular basis? Sounds like grappling could result in constructive growth.

And if you're asking something like, "Why should I deal with these Black people problems?" maybe the "why I want to grapple" behind your defensive question is, "I'd like to walk into a room with a Black person and not feel uncomfortable." Allowing that "enlightened self-interest" is a way of moving forward in a constantly changing society. There can be a personal gain woven into the willingness to show up and help others. If that desire stokes your willingness, first become aware of issues important to Black Americans. Read, watch, learn, act.

As White men, we too easily get aligned with the status quo, the dominant culture as it stands (especially because we benefit from it), and we don't always examine the deeper issues that would question how things stand. Asking why turns us inward and helps us consider our socialization, our unconsciousness, and the deeper reasons behind why we are doing what we are doing in the first place.

Agility

Agility is defined as the ability to move, think, and understand quickly and easily. Emotional agility, as we discussed before, involves seeing feelings as an opportunity to work with your emotion.

We can create agility on a daily basis, just by allowing ourselves to feel our feelings and move through them. We avoid feelings because we don't want to get stuck in them, but by avoiding them, we actually do end up getting stuck in them, which makes us more determined to avoid them next time around. It's a vicious cycle.

Better to just acknowledge it the way you do a food craving: "Hmph, I want to eat that piece of cake, isn't that interesting? Must want carbs to give me energy... maybe a walk instead." Just by acknowledging the craving I find the agility to pivot. It's typically the same with our thoughts and our feelings.

If you're dealing with a really intense emotion, though, I find it helpful to turn to Tara Brach's RAIN approach. Take it step by step and **R**ecognize, **A**llow, **I**nvestigate, **N**urture. Instead of moving away from your feelings or judging them, RAIN means first *recognizing* the feeling, then *allowing* it room in your mind. You feel it and then *investigate* it (e.g., "I'm kind of pissed off right now. Why? What's going on?") Finally, you *nurture* yourself during the experience you're having in the moment. Remember, intense emotions can feel like tigers.

The process doesn't come naturally at first since we've been so socialized to crave rapid resolution—fix it, deal with it, buck up. That's a dogma, and it's rigidity is most definitely not agility.

If you find yourself being ruthless with yourself, in addition to the keystone emotions of meeting yourself with courage and compassion, add a dash of curiosity and humility, as well. Be humble enough to accept forgiveness from yourself. You'll find it makes forgiving others more profound. And by having compassion and forgiveness for others we actually free ourselves to live the life we want. The power doesn't rest in others but in self, and that creates a capacity to show up to life that is quite powerful. Life's wind gusts don't become life's hurricanes.

Practice

The world is full of advice. Self-help books and audiobooks as a category have brought in billions of dollars. But remember: life can't be hacked through reading a book. It has to be lived. You are the canvas on which your life gets created. We have to remember that the over-dominant intellect might like you to think that the epiphany it just had is all you need to make a change. And yet far too often we stay stuck in old behaviors, the "new way of seeing something" only getting us stuck in a kind of awareness hell.

Life is, in fact, a practice. Living is a kind of practicing. We are forever at some stage of trying to figure it out. And yet, when you hear people talk about their lives, they usually skip over what's called the "messy middle." That middle is filled with a bunch of scribbles and eraser marks and sweat stains.

Their story will go something like this: "I was doing great, hit a rough patch, but righted myself. (Of course.)" The end.

I've been in a men's group for nearly twenty years, and as a group we acknowledge our own struggle with this. How can we share our struggles with one another in real time as they are happening in our lives? As is true with many men, we grapple internally and far too often, silently, until we have things figured out, and only then do we share the clarity or resolved dilemma of what has been happening in our lives. Indeed, it is deeply vulnerable to say: I'm hurting, I don't know the way out, and I need some help.

This messy middle is where we can feel a kind of clue-lessness. Too often we leave that out and just report from the place of having already resolved it, the other side, so to speak. Brené Brown calls this "gold-plating the grit." People don't share the uncomfortable, awkward nature of strug-gle. They tend to share the insights that they get *after* the struggle. They think they are sharing vulnerability, but they've already neatly wrapped it up. Real vulnerability, real openness, is revealing all of who we are, especially the parts where we don't know and maybe are scared or lonely, the parts we try to keep hidden. Too often we send a repre-sentative into the world, the one we want everyone to see. But that requires a huge amount of energy and can often leave us exhausted. Instead, grappling with the unwanted parts means we are engaged with life, we aren't on the side-lines, and yet we are naming the struggle out loud as best we can, in real time.

Getting to this point is a process. Men often start off at Step One, saying only "I'm fine." Then they might progress to the second step, which is, "Yesterday I wasn't doing well, but now I am fine." Step Three is, "I'm not doing well. I look fine, but I'm not doing well." That's when we are vulnerable; we're actually saying the problem in the moment. And then the final step is both saying and being: "I'm not doing well, here is what that looks like now, and I need help although I'm not exactly sure what that help looks like."

Socialization says that only women get to be this vulnerable. That isn't true, but it does come more naturally to women perhaps because as children they quickly learn the vocabulary of feelings and are allowed to admit them. This being the case, it sometimes helps men to practice being vulnerable with women first. One way to do it, psychologist John Gottman advises, is for men to be open to being influenced positively by their wives as advised earlier in the book. After they're comfortable with that, the next step could be to find a community of men where they could begin to share, learn, and grow together.

In the case of the shed catastrophe, I was positively influenced by my wife after the fact when she shared the public embarrassment I had cost her and made it clear how far I had overstepped. I understood then that the shed was not *my* property—it was *our* property.

Practice can be messy. It is also the way we get better at life. Better, not perfect. Voltaire said perfect is the enemy of the good, meaning that by striving for something that lives in the impossibility of perfect and being stuck in that pursuit, we rob ourselves of showing up to the good and the movement that is created when we let go of the constraints of pursuing perfectionism.

Paradox

We've touched on this before: the multiple angles, sides, opinions, and truths, to any situation. And sometimes those truths are in seeming direct opposition to one another. Recognizing this is a sign that you are grappling. Conversely, if you never recognize paradoxes in your own life and in the world around you, that's a sign that you're probably not grappling.

In terms of current events, paradox has its benefits. We're socialized to only see two sides to complex issues like enslavement. Consequently, we ask oversimplified questions that reflect our simplistic black and white take of it's either this or this. For example, let's look at the issue of reparations: Do we pay reparations to the descendants of slaves, or is that giving people handouts that will disempower them? Reducing a complicated issue down to one thing or the other creates a kind of emotional comfort, a kind of security that reassures us we're not about to be taxed intellectually or emotionally. But of course, it's a false security that overlooks nuance and subtleties and the uncomfortable sense that there may be no one "right" answer.

Another example is the All Lives Matter movement. John Stewart recognizes the power of paradox when he states: "You can truly grieve for every officer that has been lost in the line of duty in this country and still be troubled by cases of police overreach. Those two ideas are not mutually exclusive. You can have great regard for law enforcement and still want them to be held to high standards." Recognizing competing angles that must be integrated and synthesized through grappling is one of the benefits of paradox.

Researchers believe there are creative advantages to the ability to accept and reconcile paradoxes. They also measure people's ability to process such information in a concept called "integrative complexity"—the ability to accept that there are multiple ways to look at an issue and that all of these ways are legitimate; along with the ability to link these and blend them into an overall judgment.

My favorite paradox is this: Life is amazing, beautiful, profound, and powerful. It offers moments I can't adequately describe, like seeing my daughter born as the sun rose. And yet life is also full of terrible moments and struggles, moments like seeing myself in the newspaper, the divorce that ended my first marriage, and seeing disappointment in my children's faces when they have made a mistake. We know life is hard, but it's neither good nor bad. It's both. It's all. Life is sacred and profane. Wonderful and tragic. Uplifting and humbling.

Life can also merge wonderful and terrible moments at once, such as the life-changing birth of my first child when I was overwhelmed and distracted. If I had been grappling, I would have said, "I'm feeling melancholy over the end of my childless life. Everyone is acting like it's this joyous event and wondering why I'm not. I can't feel joy. I'm feeling sad. I'm checking out."

If we don't hold the paradox of life, we end up creating a kind of forced polarity of either/or that doesn't reflect the deep and nuanced truths that lie in both extremes.

Here's another paradox to contemplate. The minute that you know that you don't know is actually when you know more. As Carl Jung said, "The paradox is one of our most valuable spiritual possessions," and, "It gives a more faithful picture of the real state of affairs."

Learning

Learning is a lifelong lifestyle if you grapple. It's about putting yourself in uncomfortable situations until they become comfortable because you've learned. The *New York Times'* 1619 project about slavery put a lot of people in uncomfortable positions, which became learning opportunities. We felt upset as we read more about slavery than we knew, but then we got comfortable and gained more mastery over ourselves and our opinions. We were re-formed as we learned, able to understand and value the perspectives of Black people. It was a much deeper form of learning that points to successful grappling. Early in our lives, we learn truths that end up being exposed as falsehoods more and more. We must consider that just as in life we learned those, then we can unlearn them.

Self-judgment and self-recrimination, while an early effort to fix a mistake, actually robs us of important information in learning and growing. Ironically perhaps, but a deeper acceptance of the mistake allows for more understanding of how and why it happened. That information can be used to add context and important data that will help us choose a different way going forward.

Here's a phrase for you: "fucking first time" (FFT). Whenever we do something for the FFT it can be scary and uncomfortable. This is particularly true for anyone who is a perfectionist. But doing something for the FFT is just part of the normal—the necessary—process of living, loving, and learning.

The need to learn, and the consequence of refusing to, takes me back to that quote: "In times of change, learners inherit the earth, while the learned find themselves beautifully equipped to deal with a world that no longer exists."

That's where former President Trump lives, presiding over a world that's past. He does not digest what's actually happening and he encourages his followers in the folly of this.

Which brings me to the last tactic in the Grappling Game Plan:

Equity and Justice

As White men, we have long been at the top of the food chain. Unfortunately, that has led to us not being invested in change as much as we should be. Why would we disturb our comfort? But in fact we have a responsibility to be advocates of change. We need to help create a more just and equal world. We've inherited the most from our social construct and continue to be disproportionally rewarded, while everyone else is to one degree or another penalized for not being one of us.

My friend and colleague in this work, Lee Shainis, the co-founder and executive director of Intercambio Uniting Communities, tells the story of being in a citywide meeting where he was one of the only White men in a room of twenty people. In the middle of the meeting, someone turned to him and said: "Lee, that is why you as a White male need to speak up on these issues. We are marginalized by the unconscious racist belief that goes like this, 'Well of course you would say that because you are Black,' or 'She's probably just saying that because she is a woman.' But when White men speak up, others, including White men, listen, so please, Lee, we need your voice."

When White men address an issue that doesn't involve them directly, they are perceived as neutral and that, in turn, creates a more powerful impact, especially with other White men who are listening. Lee mentioned walking away from that meeting with a new understanding of what it means to be a White man and the power he has in that role.

We are the ones who stand in the way of equity and justice being realized. We're in control of all the levers of our society's power. Yet we still tend to expect the people we disenfranchise to, by themselves, drag all of society into an inevitable future where White men are "merely" equal. As men, we've either resisted change or gone along with it, but we have not been its leader. Grappling will give us the agility we need to work proactively toward achieving this equity and release our ongoing complicity.

Having been trained to shape the world to our liking, and to have experienced how lucrative that is, it's understandable many of us have been dragging our heels. But developing a renewed (or new) sense of compassion for self creates a deeper empathy for others. Understanding the experience of marginalized groups allows for a richer experience for ourselves. And yet compassion also lets us see the subtle ways we hold onto power, refusing to let it go "because others aren't doing it right."

For example, too often as White men we have looked at those protesting the status quo power we hold, and we have found fault in their way of protesting. Instead. if we could step out of our experience and into the shoes of others not like us, we would know the truth in what author A.

M. Leibowitz meant when she said, "This is literally what it's like to be a part of a marginalized group. Politeness is met with refusal to listen, anger is met with demands for politeness." We have to come to terms with the voices of the oppressed in whatever form or feeling they might be expressing. And we must hold compassion for ourselves as our eyes and hearts are opened.

Oftentimes, we say we have someone's back as a gesture of goodwill in a friendship. But what would it be like if we had our own back? What's possible if we stood up to the attacks of shame and blame that we heap on ourselves by having our own back? Roshi Joan Halifax has a saying that goes "strong back, soft front." Too often we end up with a sort of weak spine and an armored front. This backfires on us as it can only serve to alienate us further from the people and the life we want.

You could start by refusing to stay silent in the face of sexism. Just call it out instead. We men just don't do that. In fact, instead of calling out sexism, we come to one another's defense and excuse it, perpetuating a false male intimacy that comes from marginalizing and sexualizing women who become the "other." This can create a bond between those who share an enemy. Men connect this way around the oppression and sexualization of women. It's painful for me as part of the paradox that I have to live into: I have to own my masculinity in all its gifts and goodness, while at the same time navigating the tension of knowing the cost of unrestrained and toxic masculinity on our world.

You could also grapple through equity and justice by seeking opportunities in your own lives to call out our brothers who are engaging in racism. It doesn't mean attacking them. Remember, compassion. When GOP Rep. Yoho called Democratic Rep. Ocasio-Cortez a "fucking bitch," many men came to Yoho's defense saying, "He's a good guy." Can't he be a good guy who simply has to own his socialized sexism and his unconscious discrimination? Can't his defenders call on him to do better?

After the Ocasio-Cortez incident, I asked my wife and a few other women whether they had ever been called the same insult, and I was appalled when they all said, "Oh, yeah." Anyone who is part of this status quo, who makes mistakes like Yoho's, should not sit in denial mode. They should see these mistakes as an opportunity to say, "Yeah, I was part of that, and I regret what I said. This is what I wish that I had done. This is what I do now."

We need to learn to leverage our privilege. Ocasio-Cortez, for instance, would be a great president because she knows how to tangle in the male-dominant world. But she can't do it alone. She needs our help to change the status quo.

And we have to come to terms and own the biggest racial justice paradox of our country—that we are founded as a democratic nation built by the slave labor of stolen Africans. That acceptance lays a foundation for building change.

PRACTICAL ADVICE

When you're in the midst of grappling in real time, trying to take action on hard issues, it can be a complex and confusing proposition. You have the basics of grappling already, but as you advance, it helps to have some tactics and tips you can use according to need.

Reframe Learning

Sure, we men are ready to learn when it comes to our careers or our passion for fine wines or any of those things that further our ambitions whether professional or personal. But, as we talked about, mostly we've been conditioned to be know-it-alls, to have the opinion that matters most in the room. We don't want to take a demotion to student, even student of life. Even the word learning rubs some of us the wrong way.

It's time to reclaim the natural sense of excitement and wonder that we used to feel when we were learning. Hell, all our play as children was just learning in disguise. Remember how it felt to know you were going to get to learn to drive? It was a skill that was going to lead somewhere—to dates and road trips and freedom. Learning is fun, even if it sometimes requires a lot of effort. Learning is a door opening.

Still, it may help you to reframe the notion of learning and even the word itself as something that resonates better with you. Are you into fitness? Maybe you'd like to think of yourself as training. Are you an explorer? By all means, explore. Discover, uncover, master—think in ways that replace negative connotations with positive ones. Give yourself every edge in your grappling. Embrace the adventure that your life is.

Lean into Your Successes

While replacing the negative with the positive gets rid of some of the internal friction we feel around learning, it can't relieve us of the very real work that grappling requires. It can feel like a Herculean task in the moment, and to bolster yourself, recall a particularly hard situation you resolved, or an obstacle you overcame. It doesn't matter if it relates to what you're currently grappling with. And you're grappling with something unfamiliar, otherwise you wouldn't feel such growing pains.

If you know you're going to face a formidable situation, forearm yourself by recalling past situations where you learned, you overcame, you emerged from difficulty wiser and stronger. Calling on the ability to see something through, to endure, to show grit and courage—remembering times you brought your strength and character to bear—summons them for you in real time. Relive these successes in your mind, feeling how you called on inner resources, remembering the feeling afterward. Gather yourself, the best of you, and bring that forward with you. You are writing your own story here and that is an important piece of how we wire in continued success.

Meet Emotion with Emotion

To we men, confrontations with sexism and racism can often feel punitive, as if something is being done to us. By now you realize that this feeling arises from knowing we're the beneficiaries of an unjust cultural construct. Of course, it makes us uncomfortable, as if we, personally, are perpetrators no matter how much we've tried to avoid being part of the problem.

A strategy for dealing with difficult, intense feelings is to meet emotions with something other than the intellect. Since these deep emotions are impenetrable to reason, Canadian psychologist Leslie Greenberg says, the best way to change an emotion is *not* to meet it with logic. It's to meet it with another emotion. Instead of analyzing or arguing or trying to refute your big feelings, keep yourself in the realm of emotion. Confront your feelings with a different emotion. When you are simmering with anger, what if you breathed and remembered the peace of that walk in the woods you had? What if you met sadness with nurturance? Or intense shame with compassion? You're not trying to discount the emotion; you're trying to redirect it with kindness toward a more productive place that enlarges perspective.

Some emotions are harder to counter than others. One example is loneliness. Though men are deeply lonely, we tend not to realize it. We have been disconnected or only semi-connected for so long, it feels normal even if "bad." If you don't know what to do with a feeling, it's okay just to just let it linger there. Feelings don't last forever. Remember: after ninety seconds the chemicals the emotions caused are gone. If you continue to feel fear, anger and so on after a minute and a half, look at the thoughts that you're thinking that are stimulating the emotional looping circuitry.

Set Boundaries

The word "boundary" gets thrown around a lot in a self-help culture. What it really means is that you have sole agency over your own words, behavior, and interactions, and that you choose who you engage with, when that engagement happens, and what it looks like. Boundaries create a safe and sacred space that you walk around with all the time. From within your space, you can lead with an open, generous heart, living with integrity.

Boundaries are a must. Without them, we run the risk of becoming victims or martyrs. We open ourselves up to feeling resentful, put-upon, disgruntled, bitter. We close our hearts. Often, we end up acting on things we don't believe. Our internal world no longer matches our external world. It can't.

Breached boundaries cause you to act from early learned responses that may have helped you survive, but they do not reflect your true self. When you can determine your boundaries, they reflect your values. When you maintain them, you show your integrity and self-respect. And they keep you centered when the call to a possible crisis would otherwise make you sidestep the opportunity.

But boundaries have to be built and maintained consciously. Some of us only have strong boundaries around us to keep others out and keep our feelings in. They are more protective than they should be. What would an authentic boundary look like? Feel like? You can explore that through introspection and retrospection aided by your heart. When a situation doesn't feel good, you can look back on it later and recognize, "That didn't feel good. That's a boundary for me right there. What will I do next time to uphold my boundaries and values?"

If someone says a racial slur in front of you and you weren't happy with how you froze, you find another value-based boundary. Going forward as the proponent of healthy change in the world, what boundary will you set the next time?

By grappling with our emotions with compassion and courage, tolerating discomfort, and growing our own emotional capacity, we can begin to hook into our more whole and human selves and dismantle the societal construct and role we've been playing. The wattage inside us becomes more than the small bulb of the role, and we can shine brighter as ourselves.

THE GRAPPLING JOURNEY

Tiring but Familiar	Enlivening but Awkward
Pushed toward Change	Seeks Change Intrinsically
Answers	**Questions**
Go It Alone	Cultivate Community
Need to Be Right	**Practicing to Get It Right**
Reactive	Creative

EMOTIONAL FRAGILITY

AFTER

BEFORE

EMOTIONAL AGILITY

Knowing	Learning
Good versus Bad	**The Paradox Adventure**
Return to the "Way It Was"	Change Is Only Guarantee
Self-Punishment/Shame	**Compassionate Accountability**
Doing	Being

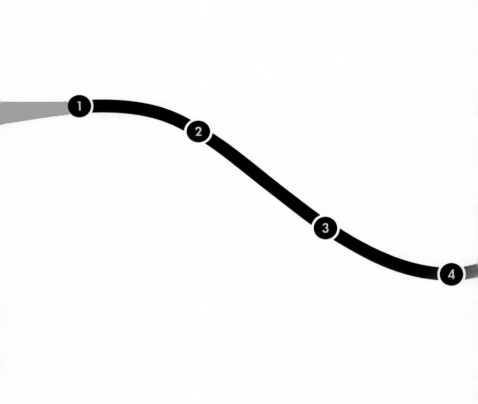

7

GRAPPLING IN THE BIG THREE ARENAS
PERSONAL, INTERPERSONAL, AND SOCIAL

"...A miracle is taking place. A continent of new common ground has emerged from beneath the waves where there are twenty, thirty, forty million White Americans saying, 'Racism is real, more real than I thought. There's something wrong with our justice system. It's more broken than I knew. What can I do about it?'...(Beginning to cry) Much more is possible than we had dared to hope for. Somebody killed a Black man and everybody cares...Somebody killed a Black man and everybody cares. I wish my parents were here to see it."
—Van Jones, after the 2020 death of George Floyd

Van Jones's moving remarks amid the growing swell of support for the Black Lives Matter movement encompass the three major types of grappling: personal, interpersonal, and social. As he spoke, the prominent Black commentator grappled personally to changing events: he, like others, has spent a lifetime feeling that only fellow Blacks would be outraged about a Black man being killed by the police. He has long felt that White Americans don't take those killings seriously.

But change burst through, change Jones wouldn't have predicted. Protests against George Floyd's murder broke out across the country, attended by a spectrum of cultural demographic representatives. Jones saw them come together to grapple interpersonally, different groups finding unity behind a common cause. And that interpersonal grappling turned to societal grappling, the protesters demanding a reckoning with the forces of injustice and racial inequity. The protests saw White Americans express unprecedented levels of public outrage over the killing of a Black man, and that outcry profoundly moved Van Jones.

Speaking about all this, Jones wasn't afraid to grapple with all this and his own emotions in real time and on the record. His open message moves those of us who watch the video, a man showing power and gravity through the profundity of his heart at this moment in our nation's history.

Jones also demonstrated aspects of grappling that we White men have not excelled at—transparency and authenticity. Jones reveals truth, the truth of what he sees, the truth of what he feels, the truth of what it could mean in the greater scheme of things for our society. In doing so, Jones leads the way for others to do the same.

It's my wish that all of us socialized White men could grapple as Jones does, revealing the dignity and power of human authenticity, and do it throughout our life.

The three big arenas of grappling are interconnected. We grapple privately with ourselves in reaction to a trigger. We can grapple interpersonally as we discuss the trigger with others. Or perhaps others *are* the trigger we are struggling with. This grappling can often culminate in societal grappling, looking at ourselves as part of a collective formed by the societal forces we help shape. We live in these three arenas and so we grapple in them. And often our grappling overlaps from one arena to the next. If you persist in moving from fragile to agile, life in real time will influence you as it did Van Jones. And when you grapple spontaneously your ability to grapple will in turn influence others and move them, as Van Jones does. As a maturing grappler, you'll ask yourself, how does the changing world change me, and how does the changing me change the world?

DON'T REINVENT THE WHEEL

Grappling in each of the three arenas may sound daunting, but it's important to realize that you've already been through plenty of times in your life when you've adjusted to a new paradigm and become comfortable in it. You've got the basics of grappling now and have begun practicing it, relying on learning and feeling. Slowly, but surely, you're going to build on that foundation to grapple in harder areas and to grapple in the moment.

And you can do this and do it increasingly well. In fact, if you've succeeded anywhere in life, you've already successfully grappled. This is just a matter of adjusting what you know to a different circumstance, the circumstance of life. You can bring your existing experiences to the grappling journey. For instance, transfer skills you have developed in your professional life. You know how to apply yourself, challenge yourself, engage in critical thinking, sit with a problem until you make a wise leadership decision. Do the same in leading yourself away from your conditioning and toward an actualized you.

Say your sales numbers were down this month. You would troubleshoot: What could you do differently to meet customer demand? What kind of market research could you do? How could you gather your team to put your heads together? All of these strategies can be transferred over to grappling, using the grappling hook of learning.

And then you'd adapt, wouldn't you? You'd listen to your customers and study what innovative competitors are doing. You'd make shifts in your business that might be uncomfortable, but you'd tolerate it instead of getting frustrated. Why? Because you know uncomfortable conditions aren't forever. Eventually, the unfamiliar becomes the familiar. You will be comfortable in this new paradigm. You would practice high frustration tolerance until that happened.

You don't have to reinvent the wheel. This is about putting your existing grappling in areas that you previously wouldn't have done. You'll dare to name and feel your emotions for the elevated cause of becoming whole. You'll own and name your socialized assumptions for the good cause of expressing your true identity to others and forming deep and meaningful relationships. And you'll engage in a reckoning with the cultural effects of White male dominance for the sake of helping to create a society that gives all people the privilege of living in pursuit of their best selves. Bring your grappling skills over from sports, hobbies, relationships, hardships you've overcome and the like. Put them to work for a good cause.

LEARNING TO ENGAGE IN ANY ARENA: THE GRAPPLING TRIANGLE

All of this advice is intended to set you up for learning to engage anywhere, in any arena any time. Personal.

Interpersonal. Societal. You can think of them as a trian-gle, upon which all grappling you do in one arena touches another. When you grapple successfully with an internal issue it will benefit your grappling efforts in the interper-sonal and societal spheres. Likewise, grappling well with a relationship issue enriches you and increases your ability to bring that to the wider world. The microcosm reflects the macrocosm and vice versa. That means awareness of some-thing in one arena can give you insights into another.

In the real world, feeling powerlessness in your marriage might cause you to consider those who might feel power-less in your workplace. Then, you might furthermore real-ize that women and people of color must feel this way in society. Or the other way around. You might see an incident involving powerlessness in larger society and consider it also through the lens of your relations and powerlessness you yourself have felt in the past.

It might feel strange to do this reflection, much less do it on purpose. Men have been trained and socialized to compartmentalize feelings and experiences—both our own and others'—and even to regard both with a certain callousness. The Grappling Triangle reminds us to integrate experiences in all parts of our lives, to allow each to inform the rest. Thinking this way not only lets you introduce greater perspective to your grappling, it rounds your life, providing you with wholeness.

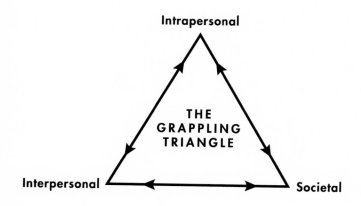

Deconstruct to Reconstruct

You may be wondering how to actually mine insights from real-life situations. Yes, sometimes chestnuts do fall from above, knocking you in the head, but if the local squirrels have been hiding nuts, you'll have to seek them out. Deconstruction can be a good place to start.

Let's say you've had a dispute with your wife. Zero in on that, forgetting any other arenas but the interpersonal one. Deconstruct first what was said. Perhaps she has been saying that you've been judgmental or critical. Unpack that with her. What did she notice that shows you this way? What are some examples? What was happening at the time? How did it feel to her? These answers deconstruct words like critical, giving you smaller, but important things to consider.

Now ask yourself questions to probe how this behavior shows up in other aspects of your life, starting with the personal. Are you talking to yourself in a judgmental and critical way? How and when did you start doing that? What triggers it? Has your socialization played into that?

Do you judge others at your workplace or in your circle of friends? What about others in society that you don't know personally? See if you can find a through line in the other areas of your life. You know the saying: "How we do one thing is how we do anything." If you were able to chart them on that Grappling Triangle, you'd see how they move back and forth through all the arenas unless you make a change. Once you realize the connections, you can start to make progress on all fronts. By deconstructing something in any area of your life, you can reconstruct, building in new behaviors based on what you've learned and how you want to show up in the world.

But right now, let's examine each arena on its own.

Personal Grappling

The most natural place to start grappling is with yourself. The unique thing about personal grappling is that you always have access to yourself, so you can do this any time, whenever it works for you. The more you do it, the more you'll get better at grappling in other areas.

All of us can find many issues to practice personal grappling. If you want freedom, wholeness, a connection to the real you and the real world, though, and a sense of efficacy in the world, your practice ought to target your socialization as a White male. It's the only way to go from fragile to agile, number one, and number two, you'll find that many of the issues in your life—for some of you, all of them—stem from your conditioning. Best to go to the source. Your rich internal world is a powerful source of information to mine.

Introspection and Retrospection

Thinking some more about how you have shown up in the world, knowing again that your behavior has been learned in the context of a patriarchal White supremacist system, it's time to consider how your true values lose out to those your socialization makes you live out. Part of the way you've been socialized is to ignore socialization, to not think about how you've been the product and the beneficiary of that system. Have you turned the channel when protests come on? Have you decided not to watch a show or a movie with a largely Black cast because you feared it would touch on present controversies or because it just didn't "seem interesting"? Do you laugh in knowing ways with your buddies when they make safe sexist small talk about their wives spending all their money?

Part of our socialization is to think we are the norm and all else a deviation. Insulating ourselves from "all else" is one of the ways we deny the wholeness of others and diminish their roles in society. It's also a way to pretend we are not actually within a system that is hurting others, that we aren't participants and that we are exempt from caring to the point of doing something about it. Part of being a good citizen in this country is realizing that what we may or may not think is our fault is still our problem.

As the women's movement grew in the sixties and seventies, there was a corresponding backlash from the White male establishment. In her 1991 book *Backlash*, Susan Faludi identified this not as a conspiracy but as an "encoded and internalized, diffuse and chameleonic" movement against the changes happening. That backlash movement exists today for those who don't like the racial progress we've made as a country. It is appropriately called a "whitelash." Larger change in society is always met with resistance by those who only want things to stay as they are.

Agility

Some people fear that endless adaptability and agility will exhaust them and burn them out. Sure, if you are agile and adaptable on a path for which you're not properly prepared and equipped, it will be a workout. Agility is not only sustainable, it's productive and efficient. Agility comes from developing balance and using judgment in real time. In this way, it's like surfing a wave. You never know exactly how a wave is going to move, so you must be responsive, leaning forward or back or to the side as the situation evolves. The wave changes, and you change as a result. You accept there is no point to try to control the wave. Instead, you respond to it. You become a student of the moment and bring yourself to the response.

This is much different than you're used to. Socialization involves pre-programmed reactions, attitudes, and beliefs, hardly conducive to agility on the fly. Attempting agility in such conditions is indeed exhausting. Pre-programming doesn't make room for an unfolding and adventurous life. It has to limit your range of experience if it is to remain in charge. In other words, for socialization to stay in place, you have to stay in your place. You must remain fragile. You have a choice. Invest in yourself through the growth gained through grappling so that you can live in an ever-changing, growing world. Or you can double down on your socialization, limiting yourself to a more mechanized and choreographed life, sheltering yourself from the dynamism the world has to offer you. When you grapple in the personal arena, you choose the dynamic world that holds surprises, the one where you hold an important place, choosing your own viability and growth.

One particular feeling poses problems to our grappling efforts—fear. When agilely responding in the moment, it will be natural to sometimes feel exhilaration, but also fear, especially if you are new to living this way. We tend to engage and attack the fear or try to repress it. Not acknowledging fear can be quite dangerous. It creates a sensation in our body that tries to help us grapple with what comes next.

Sometimes, though, there is no next. You feel fear because you've left your comfort zone. Observe the fear instead of running from it. Congratulate yourself as you summon your own resolution to bolster your courage. This keystone emotion will allow you to keep moving forward.

Remember the keystone emotion of compassion as well. Self-compassion is called for as you grapple. As French dramatist Pierre Corneille once said, "Self-love is the source of all our other loves." The better you get at loving yourself, the better you get at loving others. If you give yourself compassion instead of judgment, then you can give nonjudgmental love to others. That emotional stance adds to your balance and agility as you grapple in the interpersonal realm.

Interpersonal Grappling

Grappling is about repair. When you grapple in real time with a person, you can repair some previous damage. I know this firsthand: I grappled with my relationship with my ex-wife on a podcast I used to have. Even though we were no longer together, I wished I had been different in our marriage, and I shared my regret. I was nervous going in. How the hell would this go given we hadn't spoken in a decade? It proved to be a valuable and fun conversation. I learned some things, reconnected to this person I once walked down the aisle with, and standing up at the end of the recording, felt lighter and almost giddy at what we just did.

Whether the behavior we regret was a minute ago or 400 years ago, when our culture made the decision to enslave others and drag them from their homes, it's never too late to look truth in the eye. It's never too late for an apology. It's never too late for repair and healing.

Let Yourself Be Influenced

Men need to be more open to being influenced. That's not part of our centuries-old socialization: if the world is to be made in our own image, where would influence come in? This centuries-old socialization with us as the god of everything is how we end up trying to describe the female experience or the Black experience—even though we are the least qualified people to be able to do this.

Our relationships call us forth. Allowing your closest, most intimate relationships to give you honest, present feedback can be seeing yourself in a photograph you didn't pose for. They can see patterns and characteristics in you that you might not be aware of. They can help you understand when you are falling into a trap of socialized maleness.

Grappling's power can be enhanced by letting people have such honest conversations with us. A buddy in my men's group once gave me an unvarnished opinion on how my principles were connected to the fact that I had family money. It was easy for me to espouse certain things because I didn't have to worry about financial ramifications such as losing my job. In that moment, I was uncomfortable and self-conscious. It wasn't the first time I've faced that money privilege shame: I've done so ever since I knew the income existed. But he was right. If we don't get honest feedback from the people close to us, where will we get it? He told it to me as it was, and in that way he had my back. Many of us think listening and relating to others makes us weak. But being strong means being open to what others have to say, being curious, and allowing ourselves to be shaped by our interpersonal relationships.

I'm grateful to have friends and colleagues who have been willing to offer constructive criticism. I'm grateful for their feedback and grateful for the internal constitution that grappling has given me. That constitution has allowed me to digest and learn from the feedback I have received, including that day in men's group.

Many men try to marginalize the person who's most able to give it to them straight: their wives. Men will reject their observations, saying, "No one else has this issue with me. This is the only relationship where this is a struggle." Well, this statement itself is the opposite of grappling, because an intimate partnership asks more of us than any other relationship out there. Of course, it brings unique challenges.

Other men don't care to listen at all, as if everyone would be better off if she'd just stop talking. When this happens in therapy, I like to point out, "Look, on some level, you have to be accountable to your partner's experience of you. You can tell us that you think she's making it up or overdramatizing it, but her experience has value and you have to admit that. You can't just dismiss her experience, no matter what you think of it." This is that form of paternalism that puts men at the center, with everyone else satellites, just a prop to his importance. You may be at the center of your own experience, but you're not the center of the world no matter what the world has led you to believe through socialization.

You simply can't grow without other people. Input from your partner should not be viewed as someone trying to put a chink in your armor. Men tend to take things very personally, accusing their partners of harping on or badgering them, and sometimes they externalize it and use it as a kind of blame boomerang back to their partners. But if you frame what you are hearing as an opportunity for growth and learning, as kind of exposing an underdeveloped underbelly, this whole process can be incredibly productive.

Most of all, we need to keep the connection to others alive on this journey. It is hard enough to do by ourselves.

We have to curate a community of learners and seekers and those who are taking action to make a better world. We have to interrupt the staunch individualism so ingrained in us and reach out to those around us on the path. It might seem like you are the only one, but as you enter further into this, it will be like your eyes are getting used to the dark. You see the people that have been there all along, doing the work that perhaps you never noticed previously. These people are your allies. Connect with them intentionally and with purpose. Priya Parker creates a compelling argument for the power of getting together in her book *The Art of Gathering*. She makes the case for "crucible moments" and the sharing of intimate stories that make you change the way you viewed the world.

If you're struggling with this, that may be a signal to go back to some personal grappling—what is going on inside you? How and what is the role you're playing in it? Identify what needs grappling. Is it an issue that requires some personal growth? Have you stumbled on something that requires personal therapy or coaching? If your sense of internal knowing doesn't unearth the problem, a sense of increasing discomfort as you get close to it likely will.

Make Mistakes in Real Time

The movie *Groundhog Day* sums up interpersonal grappling perfectly. Bill Murray's character gets a shot at the same day, day after day, on a loop. He keeps making mistakes, but he's learning, he's growing, he's trying to get it right.

It also shows the pitfalls of grappling in real time in the interpersonal arena. You will most likely struggle at first, and that is a challenge. Expect that like Bill Murray's character, learning and growing will take day after day as you move toward getting it better. Though White men are afraid of making mistakes, gaining agility in the interpersonal arena includes stumbling and recovering, noticing when something goes wrong and when something goes right, and having the humility to not expect perfection.

One pitfall to avoid in this arena is becoming an expert on other people. People in this trap can describe their wife's behavior, ascribing motive, feelings, thoughts, weaknesses, issues. They become essentially an expert on the other person, but what they aren't an expert on is themselves. Part of this journey is stepping away, staying in our own lane. Your grappling lane is working on what you are bringing to the "we" and growing in order to contribute your authentic best to that.

The Challenge of Authentic Interactions

When I was teaching, my female supervisor called me in to give some feedback. I had struggled in my training program since I showed up underprepared. In a few presentations, I read directly from the book rather than engaging the students. The supervisor referenced a study that showed the difference between men and women at work in terms of preparation and level of confidence. She told me that men tend to underprepare but overstate their confidence, while women often overprepare and understate their confidence. "Could this dynamic be at work here?" she said. "You might want to consider it."

I was dumbfounded, fighting off shame. But I didn't get defensive. I recognized that a lack of preparation and a tendency to wing it was an old pattern of mine. I realized, "Oh my God, I am that man. I am that statistic."

For me, that was quite powerful: connecting socio-systemic statistics with my personal experience. I've come to terms with the fact that I'm a socialized White male, and so someone feeds me a societal statistic, I can see how the socialization or the data lives inside me. In this case, I could also be thankful for my supervisor's feedback, and not get defensive. Sometimes, we act out these socialization patterns unconsciously. I loved that supervisor for how she held me accountable with love.

Remember Your Socialization

It can feel laborious to constantly consider how your socialization influences your behavior, and it can be especially hard to do so in relationships. But the more you do it, the less frustrating it becomes to acknowledge. Recently I was trying to explain a dynamic in a movie to my family, and my twelve-year-old daughter said, "Dad, why are you talking so loud? We're right here. We can hear you." I realized she was right, and I also immediately realized the culprit was my masculine socialization coming out—I was holding forth. I caught on to what I was doing quickly because I had so much practice acknowledging socialization.

Intent and impact are two different things, and this is one of the hardest distinctions for men to understand and appreciate. I have to tell my male therapy patients all the time: "Your job now is not to reexplain your intent. Your job is to learn the impact you were having." How others experience things can very often be different than how we intend them. If men can begin to understand that, then they can understand why women might be taken aback by how much men raise their voices. Men also might begin to understand the ways in which they might gaslight or marginalize their partners without meaning to do so.

And hopefully, we men can then begin to see the gaslighting and sexism that occurs around them in society. We saw it in Hillary Clinton's presidential campaign, and in the stories of how women experience sexism in the workforce and in public spaces. We may even begin to recognize that White men have done harm, historically, in our world: to women, Native Americans, to enslaved Blacks and their descendants. And we can acknowledge that harm does not necessarily mean that these men are bad people, but flawed and socialized people.

Grappling in your personal life and in your relationships better prepares you for issues in society, the collective we. If you see something on the news that disturbs you, you'll be able to name the feeling and start asking questions.

Societal Grappling

Gregg Popovich, the president of the San Antonio Spurs, has spoken out on systemic racism in thoughtful ways. He's had to grapple with being the White head of a mostly Black team, and not only to understand what that means in terms of power, but also to connect with his players and get the most out of them.

One day, Popovich was watching the news, and his eight-year-old granddaughter happened to walk in at the exact time when the program began replaying video of the White policeman with his knee on George Floyd. Popovich didn't see his granddaughter until he turned around, and she asked, "Poppy, why does that man have his knee in that man's neck? What is he doing?"

Popovich turned off the TV and made what he described as a feeble attempt at explaining the situation to the girl. "Is she ready?" he thought. Then he realized, "Wow, if this is a problem for me, well, how about a Black family? How do you think they talk to their kids about this?" He confirms the importance of White men having a recognition of historic injustices that have continued to this day. Because men don't have to walk around thinking things like, "I've got to choose my route carefully" like women and Blacks do, it's easy to not have a full appreciation of the country's systemic problems.

Another example of societal grappling that unites the personal with our shared racial history is that related in *The Washington Post*. Robbie Robbins, a longtime history teacher at Concord Middle School in Massachusetts teaches curriculum that includes examining societal racism and prejudice. Students immerse themselves in difficult lessons about slavery, gaining understanding on how slavery was nurtured and expanded in the same America that championed equality and freedom.

Robbins, who is White, then discovered that ancestors in the eighteenth century owned a slave and later freed him. He was shocked, but the discovery brought the history closer. It became personal. And interpersonal as he decided to share it with his students. Grappling made him a better teacher.

You must try to hold the realities and truths of your past and your country's past. It's important. You must be more than just a "nice White person." "Nice" in this context means you're not actually engaging but sidestepping to avoid the systemic nature of racism and sexism. This is our system.

You are part of it. Indeed, we men created it and perpetuate it. It is definitely not nice.

We need to bring empathy to grappling with these social dynamics, intending to understand how others are impacted. We need to constantly ask: What's the impact of this thing I do, or this thing my country does, on a girl or a woman? What's the impact of this policy on Blacks? What's the impact of this on somebody who's marginalized in any way? Cornel West said it best when he said, "Justice is what love looks like in public, just like tenderness is what love feels like in private."

Hold yourself to account when you are exposed to something you don't know and you feel uncomfortable. Instead of sidestepping or resenting social reality's intrusion into your life, see the opportunity. Learn to pay close attention to the media and how they phrase the news. Resist ingrained expectations that everything should be phrased to cater to you. When Joe Biden picked Kamala Harris to be his running mate, I heard a journalist frame it: "Are Democrats and Republicans ready for a Black woman vice president?" Well, that sentence in itself was racist and sexist. What he should have said was: "Is our racist and sexist populace ready for a Black woman vice president?'

Resmaa Menakam, author of *My Grandmother's Hands*, writes, "A key factor in the perpetuation of white-body supremacy is many people's refusal to experience clean pain around the myth of race. Instead, usually out of fear, they choose the dirty pain of silence and avoidance and, invariably, prolong the pain."

Let us engage in the close struggle, committing to the emotional labor, of working towards clean pain rather than dirty pain.

And hold yourself to account even in familiar situations. Any broadcast sporting event will give you ample opportunities to do that. Take a second to notice, "Wow, this beer ad is really playing to my socialization." The more you've grappled with yourself and others, the more you can navigate situations in society in real time because you will have learned how to be present and take cues from other people. You'll know what's in your face and what's in your heart and what your values are, and you'll have no hesitation. You'll be free.

Let us engage in the close struggle, committing to the emotional labor, of working towards clean pain rather than dirty pain.

The Consequences of White Privilege

In 2019, a White Boulder police officer saw a Black male hanging out on a property in downtown Boulder. He rolled up on him and asked to see his ID. The Black man, Zayd Atkinson, said he was a student at Naropa, a Buddhist-inspired university in Boulder, and he was picking up trash outside his own building with a long metal claw. The confrontation escalated, and at one point, the officer aimed a gun at Atkinson. Atkinson actually asks several times, "How do you feel, officer?"

I found it so ironic that this Black man who was picking up trash in front of his residence had to ask the officer about his feelings. Eventually, a number of officers showed up on the scene. So did a White Naropa University administrator who told the officers that Atkinson was in fact a student who lived in that building and was indeed working. Though the administrator offered no ID, the officer believed her and dispersed the other officers.

Body camera footage of the incident became public, and the officer eventually resigned. This story shows White male privilege in action: The White officer felt threatened and didn't know what else to do but pull a gun. Atkinson, who was going about picking up trash, has to be the one to get the officer to grapple, and it all escalates until a White administrator just solves the problem. When you combine a lack of grappling with power, and Whiteness with maleness, you create a dangerous recipe. This is why we White men must admit to ourselves that we must help solve systemic racism. It can't just be up to the marginalized people themselves who do it at gunpoint or crying from teargas or while on the ground under officers' boots.

A Loss for Us, a Gain for Us

It's one thing for a White man to lose to another White man. That fits into our socialized narrative of "The best man wins." We are used to seeing that "best man" everywhere: in plays, in movies, and in most of the members of Congress. But then when a Black man comes along to win the presidency—the first American head of state who isn't White for the first time in our country's history—that exposed a real trigger for many White men. As the quote in many variations goes, "When you're accustomed to privilege, equality feels like oppression."

Race was experienced as a loss for many White men in terms of our level of enjoyment around our image being mirrored back to us, the White Man, top of the heap as the normal, right way of things. Many men (and women) found this unsettling, even if they supported Obama.

A lot of people would poo-poo our sense of loss. "We're going to talk about White men's loss?" they would say, scornfully, "Really? Haven't we talked about White men for centuries?" It is true that too often we center ourselves in the conversation. We make our feelings, our viewpoint, our needs dominant over others, and this White centering is costly.

But there is another truth. We men need to do the emotional labor of navigating the changing waters. And we haven't done that for centuries. That's part of the problem.

So my response is, hell, yes we're going to talk about White men. Because although we have enjoyed so much power and privilege, we have not had the space to grapple with our own emotions around the changes happening around us. And that breeds unresolved feelings, with us only grudgingly giving our power away or feeling like it's been taken from us, rather than a natural, normal and healthy progression to a better, more just society.

We also need to acknowledge that these changes can provoke feelings of resentment, worry, anxiety, or fatigue in us—loss—even as we remember that Black people and women have been waiting, are still waiting for equal representation. We have to do this in order to work with the world as it is, not the world as we would like it. We have to be able to name all that happened, to own our history in this country. Even if that history as White men includes some chapters that are sordid and full of oppression and exploitation. It is critical that we do this work. In doing it, we can write a different ending.

One of grappling's paradoxes is that it's about others as much as it is about ourselves. It's about issues in the world as much as it is about issues inside of us. That can be one of the hardest parts of grappling, to hold this multiplicity. If I can grapple with my own experience of change and process my own feelings, I can have empathy for others and realize the situation is not just about me. Then I can move beyond to consider the gains of having richer, more diverse experiences with the contributions of women and different ethnic groups. As White men, this imagined future may make us feel uneasy. But that is only because it's new to us, and our conditioning has tried to convince us that only we are supposed to hold the power and that other voices don't count as much as ours. Or at all.

See New Perspectives

Just as we men often marginalize our wives, we also tend to marginalize and label voices from outside our own group. We can dismiss a book about feminism as, "Oh, yeah, that's written by a woman, who is of course just advocating for herself." We do the same things when African Americans speak up about their own journeys. But as White men with a shit-ton of privilege, we need to stop minimalizing these views and begin listening to them.

We need to listen, read, understand, hear, and witness people's stories that are not about us. We need to listen to women and racial and ethnic minority groups. But to really listen we need to open our ears and our hearts in a way that we don't just seek the information that confirms what we already know. It has to be a discovery of new information that expands and at times confounds our paradigm. We need to understand and value others' stories as much as we do those of our fellow White men. Our group can be an ignorant one, and it simply isn't tenable anymore, not if we want to remain relevant.

We have to be able to build real relationships with people who don't look like us. But it isn't just about having friends who are Black. We have to speak up and amplify marginalized voices. To stand as an ally next to and in support of women, Black and brown people. And we do not do it from a performative place. This isn't about posting images on social media so we are seen as supportive. We do it from a deeper place of having really wrestled with hard questions and hard truths about our role in an unjust world. We use an informed voice.

That means absorbing the perspectives of Blacks like author Kimberly Jones, who has compared racism to playing a rigged game of Monopoly. She said it was like having "to play on behalf of the person you're playing against. You have to play and make money and make wealth for them, and then you have to turn it over to them." Which makes it impossible for Blacks to win.

We have to welcome perspectives like that of Audre Lorde, a Black feminist activist, who wrote *The Master's Tools Will Never Dismantle the Master's House*. I agree with that declaration. And I agree that White men can't be trusted, on our own, to create societal change for the sake of doing right alone. We're not the best with change. Until we learn to grapple, change scares us.

One of my favorite books is *A Hope in the Unseen: An American Odyssey from the Inner City to the Ivy League* by Ron Suskind. It's an inspiring book about Cedric Jennings, a boy who grew up in inner-city Washington, D.C., and, with the help of his single mom, excelled in a school where success was very hard to come by. Jennings eventually got into Brown University and struggled in college because he did not know how to navigate White culture.

We may not want to grapple with the sins of our fathers, or to feel shame or guilt. That's why it's helpful to divorce these sins from ourselves as people. However, we can't be deluded into thinking we are in a separate camp from marginalized groups. We are all interconnected. We're a collective.

That makes taking action an important step. It will mean risk, behavioral stretches that support the awareness gained from our reflections. But, as Martin Luther King, Jr. said, "The time is always right to do the right thing."

Take Care of Yourself

Questioning our identity and undoing our racist and sexist training is a tiring process. Navigating this new, changing world as White men can often result in compassion fatigue. Perhaps you are watching the news, and snap something like, "Okay, enough already. What more do you want? What more do they want?"

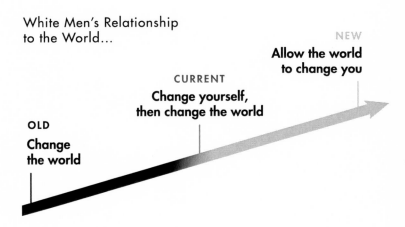

White Men's Relationship to the World...

NEW
Allow the world to change you

CURRENT
Change yourself, then change the world

OLD
Change the world

We folks who provide support in the personal growth space deal with compassion fatigue as part of our careers. We learn to feed our being and spirit in order to stay present for others. If we don't know how to restore and reconnect with our internal cores, we won't have the tolerance to navigate the pain of others. Being aware of your own compassion fatigue allows you to recognize when you're feeling annoyed and don't have the capacity to be compassionate with anyone at that moment.

Gaining agility doesn't mean you surf the waves all the time, 24/7. Agility means knowing when to stop, too. When you're feeling fatigued, act like it. Give yourself some love, fill those needs that you have. And connect it all to your body. Don't just live in your head. Self-care ultimately allows you to be more fully agile.

When you are your whole and true self in the world, you're much less likely to feel threatened as the world changes around you. You'll understand that every interaction is not a litmus test for your own worthiness. You'll get that you can have racist and sexist patterns and still be a good person. You'll have an intrinsic, sustainable confidence. You'll deliberately seek out people who are different than you, because you understand that brings more vitality to your life.

To quote William Shakespeare, "To thine own self be true / And it must follow, as the night the day / Thou canst not then be false to any man."

RETURN ON INVESTMENT: YOUR REWARD

When speaking about her own struggles and the nature of finding one's voice in life, Maya Angelou said simply, "The price is high, but the reward is great." It is hard to wade into discomfort, but we do it because it brings us a clarity of purpose that is potent. Your "reward" is also confidence, joy, love, and a sense of peace. Many of the things you want in life are gained as a reward for doing the hard work of grappling.

This gives us White men a definite return on our investment. And in this time of systemic and societal change, grappling lets us dismantle the fortresses and armor that isolate us from the real world. Grappling instead lets us change the world around us.

Activist Lynne Twist, founder of The Soul of Money Institute, says: "Our legacy is what we live—not what we leave." I say that by grappling, we leave a legacy through *how* we live out what poet Mary Oliver calls "your one wild and precious life."

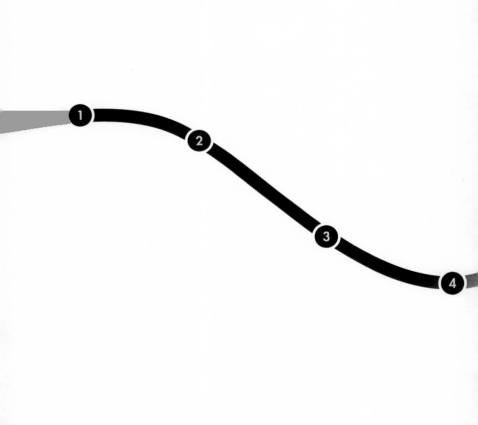

CONCLUSION

"Our deepest calling is to grow into our own authentic self-hood, whether or not it conforms to some image of who we ought to be."
—Parker Palmer

Masterful grappling means letting the world influence you so that you, in turn, can influence the world. As you continue grappling, you move from fragile to agile.

Grappling is your Hero's Journey, a calling to become who you were born to be. I've given you the tools to do this, providing the wisdom you need to fight the harmful effects of White male socialization and to do it without weapons. The rest is up to you.

For ten years, I saw therapy patients in the morning, changed my clothes, and then headed to the local high school to lead basketball practice in the afternoon. My morning required deep presence and compassion. My afternoon required an entirely different kind of energy of passion and strength. I got very good at separating these two parts of my life and bringing the very disparate energies to each.

Then, I went a step further: I learned to combine these energies. I brought the passionate assertive energy of basketball coaching to my mornings in my therapy office and called in the deep compassion of practicing therapy to my afternoons on the high school court. I noticed things started to shift, and change came quickly for my players and my clients. That dynamic, that interconnectedness of the energies we embody, is really at the heart of grappling.

This is a fight, but your only weapons are love and curiosity and compassion and humility and courage. You have to take what you already do well and use it on behalf of change and growth and learning. As James Baldwin said: "Not everything that is faced can be changed, but nothing can be changed until it's faced."

Here's what we've faced in this book:

We learned that White male dominance is a self-perpetuating system driven, in part, by White fragility and a dearth of agility. And that we—straight White Christian cisgender males—have society's golden ring. We have more privilege than everyone else, and all the outer accoutrements of that—more safety, more comfort, more opportunities, more money, more and better housing, food, health care, longevity, security, and on and on. Yet, we are less able to grapple with our feelings, less able to deal with changes in the world, less able to find our wholeness inside, less able to own and live into our full humanity. We are far from agile. In fact, after a lifetime of conditioning, we have become fragile.

Failure to have whole, thinking, feeling men damages a society in which we are the main decision makers, and it saps life essence from we men ourselves, who do not know what it is to fully love ourselves and others, not as an act of morality, but as an act of fundamental human-ness. Our society creates men estranged from themselves, which turns us into masters of inhumanity to the rest of the world.

But all is not lost. Sometimes to know something fully, we have to experience its opposite. In these pages, I've shared some very "opposite" experiences that provided me valuable lessons on how I, myself, really want to be in the world. (I won't be rebuilding any more sheds.)

Years ago, I took my six- and eight-year-old kids to the bike park here in Boulder. Off to the side of the park there is a separate area that contains a "pump track." This is a circuit of rollers and banked turns in an area the size of a basketball court. The track is designed to be navigated by pumping, generating momentum by up and down body movements, not by pedaling or pushing. It was fascinating to see the skill and agility in kids of all ages as they moved their body on the down portions to have enough speed to continue into the up portions, only to be repeated all over again seconds later. As I stood and watched, I couldn't help but think of the work I was doing in helping people navigate the downward and upward moments in their lives.

Grappling builds the muscle and that muscle creates a kind of momentum that can support greater efficiency in navigating challenging times. We can trust that we can go towards the struggle because we know how: we have experienced struggle over and over and we have come out the other side. Not only do we no longer resist struggles, but we can almost relish them because in going towards it, we feel the power of transformation calling us. Then, we can see the work we did to get where we are and know that the same opportunity to grow will be awaiting us always.

The whole experience creates the momentum that makes life work, just as at the pump track. Momentum empowers your agility. Embrace it, feel the ease and rhythm that comes from moving towards, through, and beyond challenges in your life. There is a flow that makes grappling less about work and more about being alive to the full range of what life offers us. And we can experience our own power and grace in the up and downs of everyday life.

Embrace it, feel the ease and rhythm that comes from moving towards, through, and beyond challenges in your life.

If we can embrace uncomfortable feelings of not knowing, we can relearn the excitement of discovery. We don't have to always know everything. There are big advantages to lifelong learning, for us and the rest of the world. We must resist mashing down our feelings, the too often habit of containing them, of holding them in. Instead, we must feel and engage in those feelings; learn from them and respect them. Sustaining the effort can create real change, and change within restores sight and healthy growth.

In *White Fragility: Why It's So Hard to Talk to White People About Racism*, Robin DiAngelo shared how her work has given her a new perspective on life and on herself:

It's an ongoing and often painful process of seeking to uncover our socialization at its very roots. It asks us to rebuild this identity in new and often uncomfortable ways. *But I can testify that it is also the most exciting, powerful, intellectually stimulating, and emotionally fulfilling journey I have ever undertaken.*

[Emphasis mine.] It has impacted every aspect of my life—personal and professional.

I have a much deeper and more complex understanding of how society works. I can challenge racism more often, I can challenge much more racism in my daily life, and I have developed cherished and fulfilling cross-racial friendships I did not have before.

It's a tall order. But you don't have to do it all at once. This book is a call. It's a call to be real and whole and true in the world. In steps, small steps. I have done my best to give you, the reader, some tools and practices to grapple in your own life. The words in this book are just that: words. Each of the ideas in this book are only as good as you allow them to be. Take them and go out and live your life. Ford a creek, listen to music, sit under a tree, have a courageous conversation with yourself at a stoplight. Live as yourself and let your purpose live through you from moment to moment.

The better you get at using the words in this book, really exploring these ideas inside yourself, the better you get at personal grappling, and then interpersonal grappling, and then actually effecting change in the world and society. Grappling positions you to be a voice that represents your values properly and live in brave moments. This life, your life, is a deeply personal experience. You *can* do the work of running it through your heart.

Racism and sexism aren't just suddenly going to improve. The drums of change beat louder and louder. As White men, we have to stop denying and minimizing change and instead turn and face the reality of our evolving world. The upside of all of the upheaval in our country is that it is bringing lightness to the dark. Remember again, the wisdom of Margaret Mead: "Never doubt that a small group of thoughtful, committed, citizens can change the world. Indeed, it is the only thing that ever has."

RESOURCES

Workshops

I'm partial to the experiential work as it allows for a deeper, longer-lasting understanding of concepts. There isn't a person on this earth who couldn't benefit from the Hoffman Process; it's just that good. Not easy but so worth it. I'm also grateful to PISAB (People's Institute for Survival and Beyond) for helping deepen my understanding of systemic racism and White supremacy. Couples workshops can help break down the silo experience and isolation that exists in so many intimate partnerships.

- The Hoffman Process: *www.hoffmaninstitute.org*
- Peoples Institute for Survival and Beyond: *www.pisab.org*
- Gottman Couples Workshops: *www.gottman.com*
- Hold Me Tight Workshops: *www.iceeft.com*

Websites

- Practical tools for taking action: *www.racialequitytools.org*
- Organizing White Men for Collective Liberation: *www.owmcl.org*. A national network mobilizing white men to learn, grow, and take action against White Supremacy and Patriarchy.
- *YES!* magazine: *www.yesmagazine.org*. Rigorous reporting that inspires people to build a more just, sustainable, and compassionate world.
- Yale Center for Emotional Intelligence: *www.ycei.org*
- Intercultural Competence using an inventory: *www.idiinventory.com*
- National Organization for Men Against Sexism: *www.nomas.org*

Books

- *White Fragility: Why It's So Hard for White People to Talk About Racism* by Robin DiAngelo
- *Mediocre: The Dangerous Legacy of White Male America* by Ijeoma Oluo

ABOUT THE AUTHOR

Andrew Horning is a coach and teacher at the Hoffman Institute, an organization dedicated to transformative education, spiritual growth, and dimensional leadership for those seeking clarity in their personal and professional lives. As the creator and host of the podcast *Elephant Talk*, Andrew encourages couples to have courageous conversations for the sake of a deeper connection. He's the co-host of *The Hoffman Podcast*, a keynote speaker, and a volunteer and former board chair for Intercambio Uniting Communities. Andrew earned his master's degree in clinical social work from the University of Michigan and is a former licensed private-practice psychotherapist. He lives in Boulder, Colorado with his wife of nearly two decades and their two children.